If You're In the
Driver's Seat,
Why Are You Lost?

If You're In the Driver's Seat, Why Are You Lost?

A ROADMAP TO AN
AMAZING LIFE

Dr. Lawana Gladney

THE EMOTIONAL WELLNESS DOCTOR

BENBELLA BOOKS, INC. • DALLAS, TEXAS

BenBella

BenBella Books, Inc.
10300 N. Central Expressway
Suite 530
Dallas, TX 75231
www.benbellabooks.com
Send feedback to feedback@benbellabooks.com

Printed in the United States of America
10 9 8 7 6 5 4 3 2 1

Library of Congress Cataloging-in-Publication Data
Gladney, Lawana, 1963-
        If you're in the driver's seat, why are you lost? : a roadmap to an amazing life /
by Dr. Lawana Gladney.
        pages cm
    Includes bibliographical references and index.
    ISBN 978-1-939529-08-4 (trade paper : alk. paper)—ISBN 978-1-939529-09-1
(electronic : alk. paper) 1. Self-confidence. 2. Adjustment (Psychology).
3. Adaptability (Psychology). I. Title.
    BF575.S39G53 2014
    158.1—dc23

                                                                    2013029547

Editing by Debbie Harmsen and Vy Tran
Copyediting by Alexis Kelly
Proofreading by Greg Teague and
    Christine Koch
Cover design by Bradford Foltz

Text design by John Reinhardt
    Book Design
Composition by Integra Software Services
    Pvt. Ltd.
Printed by Bang Printing

Distributed by Perseus Distribution
www.perseusdistribution.com

To place orders through Perseus Distribution:
Tel: (800) 343-4499
Fax: (800) 351-5073
E-mail: orderentry@perseusbooks.com

Significant discounts for bulk sales are available. Please contact Glenn Yeffeth at
glenn@benbellabooks.com or (214) 750-3628.

To my loving mother, Shirley:
You have given me my emotional and
spiritual grounding, and
loved me through every part of my life's journey.

To my wonderful children, Jordan, Bria, Jazzy, and Lexi:
I love you with every fiber of my being and feel honored
and blessed to carry the most prestigious title this world
has to offer: your mother.

To my angels, Charles and Chelsie:
You are forever in my heart.

Contents

Introduction: The Journey

I T MAY HAVE BEEN early morning, midday, or late evening when you came into this world, and you may have entered kicking and screaming, or you may have needed a vigorous rub to kick-start that welcoming cry. But however it happened, from that very moment, you started on your journey. The journey called your life.

Your journey started out pretty fast. Within the first few years you learned to crawl, walk, and talk; your learned your ABCs and 1, 2, 3s; and you successfully adapted to change, transitioning from mommy's milk to solid food and from Pampers to Pull-Ups. "Growing up" was pretty normal and you probably even were applauded with each new progression you made.

As you continued to grow and develop, you began to experience life's ups and downs. If your childhood was ideal, then from the ages of five to twelve, it was filled with the innocence of school days, field trips, snack times, recesses, extracurricular activities, after-school programs, and weekends with family activities, birthday parties, and sleepovers.

But by the time you hit the magical "teen" years, you probably felt a bit (or greatly) lost for the first time. Maybe you were uncertain about who you were. Maybe your friends were changing. Maybe your parents became annoying and school became a place where you "had" to go. The older you became, the more you experienced the bumps, detours, traffic jams, and road blocks, which came in the form of break-ups, family fallouts, stalls in your career, or unexpected losses. You found that events and circumstances can knock you off your feet and leave you feeling stressed, confused, and lost.

Sometimes those uncomfortable feelings don't go away easily. Perhaps you still feel lost, or maybe you feel newly lost due to something that has occurred recently in your life. Whether you're embarking on a career at age twenty-two or are seeing your children off to college at age fifty-two, you need strategies to help you get "unlost." You need help in mapping out your life's direction so your path will lead you to the life you want—to what I call "your amazing life." *If You're In the Driver's Seat, Why Are You Lost?* is here to equip you with these strategies.

The Need for GPS

I've used car and trip terminology and analogies throughout the book because the journey of life is similar to the trips that we take each day when we get into our cars. Some trips are easy and uneventful—a direct shot from point A to B, with few complications along the way. Inevitably, however, we have trips that are delayed because of unforeseen circumstances—a detour, traffic, an accident, or faulty navigation. Anyone who has experienced any of these hindrances knows how frustrating they can be, and how they can lead us into feeling stressed out and out of control. Thus, we've seen the rapid rise in ubiquity of the Global Positioning System (GPS), which has become a lifesaver for many of us.

Like so many other modern conveniences, the GPS is so helpful that we've become dependent on it and can't imagine what we did before we had a lady talking to us and telling us where to turn in 0.5 miles or how to reroute. Well, I suppose I do remember. We used "cutting edge" technology like MapQuest—just plug in an address and you'd be given the directions to anywhere in the country. All you had to do was to print out twenty pages, keep them in order, and follow them closely while driving, and you'd actually reach your destination. Compared with using a GPS, that's a lot of work. However, it still beats trying to unfold a large physical map in the car while navigating at the same time! Just think what it once took to just drive across the city to a friend's house or an appointment. It was like working through a maze. Hopefully you knew where you were going, because if you didn't, you'd have to find a phone so you could stop to call for directions.

We now live in the high-tech age where trifold maps have largely gone the way of cassette tapes and you don't have to print out directions, because you can download a navigation app to your phone. Or, even better, you can purchase a GPS to mount in your car or even buy a car that comes equipped with the technology.

Wouldn't it be great if we had a similarly helpful tool to guide us on a far more important trip: Life? Wouldn't it be great if this guide would keep us headed in the right direction, help us stay focused on our destination, and help us make sure we can get back on the right route if we get lost? Consider this book your personal GPS, a talking roadmap that will help you navigate from where you are in life right now to exactly where you want to be. Whether you are lost and wandering around without direction, or, if you've hit a roadblock, this book will help you understand how to manage your emotions, your stress, your health, and your overall life. *If You're In the Driver's Seat, Why Are You Lost?* is your new GPS for life. It's here to help you recalibrate and set off in the right direction for you.

The Voice Behind the GPS

As the Emotional Wellness doctor, I have worked with countless people who feel stressed, confused, and lost when "life events" and circumstances knock them off their feet. And, I have been able to provide empowering strategies to help my clients feel more confident and ready to be in the driver's seat of their lives. I have been fortunate enough to share this advice one on one, as well as through speaking engagements across the country, which has allowed me to share my message of taking control of our own destinies so that we can enjoy life with more than twenty-two million people.

And now I have the opportunity to help you through this book. Think of me as the voice of that nice, helpful lady behind your GPS. My aim with *If You're In the Driver's Seat, Why Are You Lost?* is to guide you through everyday challenges and to help you let go of the things that are emotionally KILLING you—the people, thoughts, words, and regrets of the past—as well as help you build a plan for your future. I have written this book to be your own personal coach that you have access to twenty-four hours a day, seven days a week. It's a practical guide with essential tools that will help you take control of your destiny. It's loaded with information, tips, and strategies that will help you learn how to tap into the power of your mind; how to control your health; and how to connect to your spirit to live the life you want. Let the advice in these pages inspire, empower, and enrich your mind, body, and spirit. Believe it in your mind, and your heart will feel it, your hands will do it, and your spirit will rejoice in it.

In order to get the most out of this book, you will need to keep a blank notebook by your side and title it, *My Journey to an Amazing Life.* Always keep it and a pen handy as you read. In each chapter you'll find a REST STOP and ROADMAP, which feature suggested activities and questions that will help you evaluate your life, change your thoughts, make plans, and execute changes that will ensure that you are driving toward your destiny. Use your notebook to record your thoughts and do those exercises.

Now, buckle up, and get ready for the ride of your life. The ride to your amazing life!

ONE

Help, I'm Lost!

Coping with a Broken GPS, No Maps, and No Directions

YOUR BIG DAY has arrived. You have been waiting for this opportunity to interview for your dream job. The interview is at 11:00 a.m. Your clock goes off at 6:00 a.m. to give you plenty of time to prepare. Although it should only take thirty minutes to get there, you plan to leave at 10:00 a.m. to allow extra time for traffic and other potential delays. You are familiar with the neighborhood where the office is located and have the address memorized. You are set. You start out on the journey to your destination and the trip is going smoothly. The traffic and other drivers are cooperating with you this morning. You are feeling good and very excited about your interview; you even smile and nod at the people in the car beside you.

You are getting close to your destination, but you can't seem to find the specific street. It was Walnut, wasn't it? You could have sworn that it was just off Brook Road. As time eases closer to 10:30 a.m., you become a little concerned. Did you pass the street and just weren't paying attention? As you make a U-turn and go back a few blocks to retrace your route, you begin to get nervous as it starts to *seem* like the street you are looking for doesn't exist. The clock is moving toward 10:40 a.m. and your body hits the panic button. You stop at the nearest 7-Eleven and hope that the cashier knows where you are. Unfortunately, he just moved to the city and doesn't have a clue. You get back in the car and sit there with a racing heart. You were sure you knew where you were going, but you are not where you are *supposed* to be. You are *lost* and you only have fifteen minutes to get to the interview. You can hardly breathe as you realize that you are not going to make it. This is your big day, yet somehow you managed to get lost and blow it. You planned for everything, except for completely and utterly losing your way. After all, no one *plans* to be lost.

Lost in "Life Events"

Webster's Dictionary defines "lost" as having *gone astray or missed the way; bewildered as to place, direction, etc.* It's a feeling and emotion that every living and breathing human being—even highly trained doctors like yours truly—has felt at some time or another.

The day I found myself lost, the sun was shining and the temperature was a near perfect 75 degrees. I remember the weather so clearly because it ended up being so starkly opposite to what the day held. It was also memorable because it was Mother's Day, and I woke up feeling so blessed to be a mom to my four wonderful kids. I was, truth be told, looking forward to being showered with affection and gratitude by my husband and children in recognition for the hard work I do as a mom. Hey, I can be queen for one day out of the year, right? My husband and I had recently been having some serious strains in our twenty-year marriage, but I was hopeful we could put our issues aside for the day.

As a family, we attended church that morning and then later celebrated with a dinner at Grand Lux, one of my favorite restaurants. Despite my earlier optimism, there was palpable tension at dinner. Shortly after we arrived back at the house, my husband went into the bedroom, took out his suitcase, and began to pack his clothes and a few of our belongings. *You have to be kidding me!* We had talked about a separation to clear our heads, but I was blindsided and hurt that he chose *this* of all days to leave. By nightfall, he was gone. *Happy Mother's Day to me!*

The next morning as the sun peered through the window and I awakened to consciousness, it took a minute to realize that I was in a big empty bed all alone. I looked around the room and saw the closet door open with empty wire hangers swaying ever so slightly from the air of the ceiling fan. A suffocating sense of anxiety came over me. After more than two decades of being married, I was suddenly alone; I was "lost" and needed help to find my way. As I lay there, thoughts and questions swirled in my head: *Where do I go from here? What am I going to do now? How am I going to handle all the bills by myself? Who's going to fix the toilet when it leaks? Who's going to kill the creepy things? Who's going to protect me?*

While these seemingly unanswerable questions bombarded me, another little voice reminded me, *Hey, I am the Emotional Wellness doctor, and I help others find their way. I usually have the answers to everyone else's problems. Surely, I can handle my own.* Well, that all sounds good in theory. Although I was a strong, independent, smart, and tenacious woman, I was still lost. Even the most sophisticated map was not going to work at a time like this—how could I plow ahead when I had no idea where I was going? I needed to get to the nearest rest stop and park so that I could regroup and reroute my direction (once I figured out my destination). Over the next few months, as my husband and I finalized our divorce, I was forced to redefine who I was; reevaluate my priorities; undo and redo my life's goals; reevaluate the past; reorganize the present; and replan for the future. Because I never imagined myself in this place, I found myself grieving the loss of dreams, dealing with a gamut of emotions, and learning how to trust myself all over again. It was a watershed moment in my life, and it made me all the more empathetic to my clients and others who have felt like they were on the right path only to be blindsided and sent dramatically off-course. Clients like Jenny, Cassandra, and Tonya. (*All names of people in the scenarios have been changed to protect privacy.*)

Forty-five-year-old Jenny called me for help after a traumatizing career setback. She had been working at her job for more than six years. She was very resourceful and dedicated, and went over and beyond everyone's expectations, but it seemed as if her manager just didn't value her potential, constantly overlooking her for promotions and raises. Although she was very good at her job, she was not happy and felt that she had more to give and that another company would value her skills more. She began to circulate her résumé, and after several months of searching, a company offered her what was basically her dream job. Finally, her potential was recognized! She turned in her letter of resignation with hidden excitement. Then, exactly one month to the day she started her new job, she was let go. Jenny was angry, humiliated, embarrassed, and confused, and she went into hiding. She was lost.

Cassandra was numb since the fateful Saturday she got the call that her husband was in the hospital. He'd had a heart attack. She rushed through traffic to get to the emergency room, unaware of stoplights and stop signs. Time seemed to stand still and speed by simultaneously. Unfortunately all the speeding didn't get her there in time to say goodbye. He had passed away before she arrived. *How could this happen*, she wondered. He had been in great health. He ran every day and had regular doctor visits. One minute he was on the phone laughing, and the next minute he was fighting for his life, and then was gone, just like that. Cassandra's world crumbled in an instant.

Tonya was crying so hard it was difficult for me to understand what she was saying. Through her muffled words and deep groans, I heard the words "breast cancer." She was under forty, hadn't had her first mammogram, and there was no family history of breast cancer. There was no reason this should happen to her. She only did self-exams because her doctor said that she should. Then she felt the lump. When she got checked out and heard the words "breast cancer," her world started spinning. *How could this be? What am I going to do? Will I be a survivor?* Tonya withdrew and became lost in being *lost*.

From a sudden loss to a health scare, all these individuals felt the overall feeling of, *It wasn't supposed to be like this.* Perhaps you can identify with such a feeling. I'd be surprised if you couldn't because at one point or another we've all faced similar difficult or uncomfortable circumstances. These situations can leave us with feelings of anger, confusion, immobilization, and, in some cases, situational depression, which unlike clinical depression, is usually temporary, but often just as debilitating.

Here are some life situations that can make us feel lost:

- Loss of a job; unemployment
- Loss of a loved one from sudden death or long-term illness
- Loss/of relationships with friends, family, or lovers
- Loss of income, investments, or property
- Moving to another city, state, or country
- Marriage
- Divorce
- Parenting
- Family challenges
- Sickness and/or disease
- Aging parents/caregiving
- Experiencing failure
- Experiencing success
- Financial challenges
- Workload
- Dissatisfaction

The question then is not how you can avoid becoming lost. The question is, once you are lost, how quickly can you find your way back? To find the answer, you must first determine whether your situation was the result of an uncontrollable or controllable event.

Uncontrollable Events

Many events in life, like those presented in the earlier examples, are ones that individuals cannot control. These types of experiences I call "uncontrollable events." They could be also placed under the "ebbs and flow of life" category. When it comes to marriages and divorces, for example, there are choices and you have a say to some degree, but because there are two people involved, you cannot control the entire situation. You can only manage your responses, reactions, and thoughts.

ROAD TO RECOVERY AFTER LIFE-CHANGING EVENTS

It's normal to feel lost when major life-changing events occur. Remember that it's possible to bounce back, but getting "unlost" will be a process. There are key factors to focus on that will help you find your way, make the transition, and deal with the issues with less stress.

1. **Allow yourself the time to feel the emotions**. You will be flooded with a plethora of feelings, and you need to walk them. It's okay to be angry or cry. These are both such natural feelings that people often try to suppress. If you are angry and need to scream, go someplace where you'll have privacy. When you need to cry, don't hold back the tears. You may think that tears are a sign of weakness, but they are not. They are actually very cleansing for the soul and body.

2. **Avoid using your energy to try to make sense of things that don't make sense**. In Cassandra's situation, for example, you can't make sense of a healthy person dying of a heart attack, or for Jenny, that she was let go from her job a few weeks after being hired. Fixating on the "why" of senseless occurrences will keep you in a stagnated mental state that will in turn keep you from moving to the healing space.

3. **Focus on the people and/or things in your life that are good**. Even in the best of times, it's good to appreciate your blessings, but it is especially imperative during difficult times that you direct your attention into a spirit of gratitude. No matter how bad the situation was, it always could have been worse.

4. **Don't run and hide**. Your natural instinct may be to go into a shell and avoid all the people that love you. You may be thinking, *It's my personal pain and I want to work through it alone*. Or, maybe you feel like you'd be bothering others. Tonya, for example, didn't want to tell her friends and family about her breast cancer because she didn't want them to worry about her. However, in times like these, you'll want to engage in the opposite thinking. The more you isolate yourself, the more prone you can become to experiencing long-term depression. Without the support, love, and encouragement of others, it will be more difficult to find your way back.

5. **Focus on and enjoy the present**. Challenging life situations have a way of giving us a different perspective on our journeys and almost force us to prioritize what's important. Make sure you enjoy and appreciate the people and things that are in your life today!

6. **Create a new normal**. When things in life change, you have to change with it. My divorce forced me to create a new way to do holidays, dinners, celebrations, parenting, etc. While it may be uncomfortable in the beginning, much of it is the feeling of growing pains. You are transitioning to a new phase of your life.

7. **Seek counseling**. Always be open-minded to the idea of counseling. We all need it at some time or another. A good counselor can help you to pick up pieces and give you a different perspective on things. I highly recommend it. Finding a good counselor is not as difficult as it may be perceived. First, ask for recommendations from your health care provider or friends who have had counseling. If you don't get any personal recommendations, go online to www.findapsychologist.com or search on Google for a counselor who specializes in your specific areas. There are thousands of mental health professionals that are available to help you find your way.

Controllable Events

While we have little (or no) control in some situations, other times we do have control. In the next group of scenarios I focus on four common, controllable categories that people find themselves lost in: yourself; addiction; relationships; or finances. It is these controllable events where we are lost because of our choices, decisions, and/or reactions to events.

Losing Yourself

Have you ever questioned who you really are or have become? This generally happens when you come to a point in your life when you feel like you have lost yourself in your work, family, culture, or social circle. The struggle with identity begins when you reach adolescence. While some are able to have a grasp on who they are becoming, it can change as you enter different phases of life. For example, when you go to college, you experience new things and people that impact your ever-changing individuality. As you grow into a career, start a family, or start a business, each phase has an effect on your identity. Feeling lost may mean that you don't know who you are any more or that you realize your identity is caught up in something or someone else.

Lisa couldn't remember the last time that she watched any channel other than Disney, Nickelodeon, or PBS. She knew every actor, character, and plot from most of the episodes on these three kid-focused channels. She longed for the days when she could sit and watch something that she truly enjoyed. She also realized that no one knew her actual name. Everywhere she went she was known as Ashley and Devin's mother. She thought back to all the parental advice she was given when she was pregnant. No one told her that she would lose her identity, not be known by her first name, and not have any room in her life for her interests and passions.

Although losing yourself in someone or something can happen subconsciously, a conscious choice happens when you realize that you don't know who you are and you choose to take steps toward finding out who you are or you continue to be lost.

This is exactly where Carolyn found herself. Her husband was a very successful attorney and she dutifully attended the social functions that her husband's job sponsored. She would get dressed up in cocktail attire and schmooze the evening away as Mrs. Campbell. As she made small talk with her husband's associates, all she heard about was the success that her husband brought to the company. She endured story after story about "Mr. Wonderful" until her jaw hurt from the smiles. Carolyn silently wondered if anyone cared about her as an individual and the fact that she worked her dream job from her home office. As she listened to Chatty Cathy to her left, talking on and on about her trip to Paris, Carolyn grew increasingly frustrated that no one seemed interested in her or her interests. When another attendee walked up and she was introduced yet again as "Ted's wife, Mrs. Campbell," she stuck out her hand and said, "Hello, I'm Carolyn." After all, she was more than just Ted's wife…wasn't she?

Does any of this ring a bell for you? Many people are lost because their self-perception doesn't match their actions and behaviors anymore, or that outwardly they don't feel like they are the person they are inside. It can be hard to remember what makes you unique or what your own individual ideas or opinions are when there is so much pressure to conform to those around you and to fit into a certain mold as "the perfect mother/father" or the "ideal husband/wife." Some people are caught up in the whirlwind of our fast-paced culture that dictates what is in, out, cool, trendy, acceptable, or the latest and greatest. If you find yourself "outside the norm," it can impact your self-esteem. Only by finding and embracing your true authenticity (which we get discuss in Chapter 2) will you be able to make the decisions that will keep you on course.

Lost in Addiction

Some people find themselves lost in self-destructive behaviors or lifestyles. The desire to alleviate misery and pain, coupled with the inability to effectively manage emotions and stress, can drive an individual to become dependent on an illicit substance or compulsive activity. This can develop into a vicious cycle because feeling lost can drive a person into these behaviors, and being trapped in the throes of addiction exacerbates the feeling of being lost, and so on. A person can become addicted, dependent, or compulsively obsessed with virtually anything. Some of the most common things that people find themselves "lost" in, are:

- Alcohol
- Drugs
- Gambling
- Sex
- Pornography
- Work
- Shopping
- Food

Rhonda couldn't believe what she saw when she looked at the picture. Surely, that woman in the photo was not her. The woman staring back at her was fifty pounds heavier than Rhonda used to be. She looked like her Aunt Lucy and not the young vibrant woman she used to be. Seeing this version of herself prompted her to reach out to me for help. She knew that she was overweight, but until she saw that picture she didn't realize it had gotten so out of control. She was stuck in a pattern. She ate when she felt good, she ate when she felt bad, she ate when she was afraid, and she ate when she wasn't afraid. She explained that food was her solace and her friend, but moreover, it had become a crutch for her. She desperately wanted to change her eating habits.

And then there was Brennon, who thought that he could handle his alcohol. He had a glass of wine in the morning, again at noon, and a stronger drink at night. Although his family became concerned, he assured everyone that he was fine and continued on his path. Eventually though, the two glasses of wine during the day became four and the one nightcap become a few. He was stuck.

When it comes to breaking addictive behaviors, there is a process. Because some addictions are physical addictions and others are psychological addictions, they will require different routes to overcome. By the time a behavior can be classified as an addiction, it requires outside help and counseling from a professional. So to get out of it, you must seek professional help. I can't adequately give you steps in this book that will help you to stop the behaviors yourself. You need to walk through it with a professional.

Lost in Relationships

Being lost in relationships encompasses many dynamics. You can be lost from the lack of a relationship with a parent, child, or sibling, or you can be lost in a dysfunctional relationship that you can't seem to get out of. Whether you're lost from the lack of a connection or dysfunction, it can be harmful.

As humans, we are from birth biologically hardwired to seek connections with other people. Our most fundamental relationship is with our parents, who establish our feelings of safety, security, and identity. If that bond is never established or is broken, children can experience despair, anger, self-doubt, confusion, suspicion, and a range of other troubled emotions, with lasting ramifications.

Growing up, Bob never knew who his father was. He constantly wondered about this mystery man. Did he look like him? Did they like the same sports or music? While he was curious about the man, he was also incredibly hurt and angry that his father apparently didn't care about him since he left his mother before he was born and never came back. All of his life, he felt incomplete and displaced with his identity. At the age of thirty-five, Bob found out who his dad was. But, did he really want to meet him? Could he forgive him? He decided not to connect with him. Meeting him could disrupt his life and while he felt displaced, he didn't want to take that risk.

While you may not have had an absent parent, you may be lost in a strained relationship with a parent, sibling, child, friend, or lover. When relationships become distant and strained, it has an enormous impact on your well-being. Whether you shut down and tell yourself, "I don't care anymore" or continue to attempt to reconcile without success, the strained relationship injures your soul and causes disappointment, remorse, and defeat.

When I heard Tracy's story, I knew immediately that she was lost in her relationship. She had been married for several years, divorced, and was living with her ex-husband again. She had left her husband and sent him to prison for hurting their daughter. However, when he was released after serving his sentence, she accepted him back into her life, caging herself into the prison of the relationship. She could see that she was lost and that the relationship was not good for her, she just didn't know how to free herself.

Breaking from a dependency like that won't happen overnight. When a person is lost in another person, it is like an appendage of your body and soul, and it's difficult and painful to cut ties. Chapter 9 is devoted to ways to deal with toxic people and relationships—it's *that* important.

Lost in Finances

We may like to think otherwise, but in many ways money is the defining factor in life. It shapes your:

- Options
- Lifestyle
- Friendships
- Social class
- Tax bracket
- Housing
- Education
- Freedom
- Relationships

As you see, it is the foundation to most of life. While those who have money proclaim that it doesn't buy happiness, those who don't have it would like to test that theory. Because money is the driving force, the lack thereof has the power to significantly influence your thoughts, confidence, relationships, and identity. Financial strain can make you feel less than, angry, unworthy, embarrassed, and helpless. Conversely, wealth can make you feel unsatisfied, guilty, empty, and distrustful. Whatever the case, money is a big influencer in terms of the direction of your journey in life.

Some people have bought into the theory that they don't have control over how much money they make and believe that only certain people are designated to be rich. That is unfortunate, because as with the other things in your life, you are always in the driver's seat. Again, because this topic is critical to your life, health, and well-being, Chapter 12 addresses it in much more detail.

Don't Get Stuck

Sometimes we don't realize or don't acknowledge that we're lost, and so we stay lost, and what's worse, we get "stuck" there. There are several types of people who are stuck and can't seem to reroute.

Stubborn Sam is always lost and stays that way because he doesn't acknowledge that he is lost and refuses to ask for help or directions.

Persuasive Polly has the skill to convince everyone that she isn't lost. Although you can see her "driving around" aimlessly, never going anywhere, she seems to have persuaded herself and others that she knows where she's going.

Fearful Fred is afraid to be on course. He has become comfortable living life in a disoriented state and is content to be displaced.

Sad Sabrina likes the attention that she gets when she acts confused. She has gained the reputation of being adrift and is not happy unless she is sad.

I am certain that you have seen yourself in this chapter in one way or another. It's all but impossible not to get lost in your life. No one is spared. This chapter's exercises take a look at your own experiences with getting lost and review some helpful strategies to find your way back. As I mentioned in the introduction, each chapter will have a "REST STOP" portion, and this is the time to get out your *My Journey to an Amazing Life* notebook; it should be new and empty, ready to fill with your notes from the exercises.

Your first task is to reflect on the following questions and write down the answers in your notebook:

- Which life events have left you with this feeling of being lost?
- How long have you felt off track?
- What have you done thus far to cope?

As you review your events and the ways you've coped and are currently coping, consult the directions below and see how you can take control of the wheel again and change your direction. Remember, no one controls your destiny but you. You and only you are in the driver's seat setting the course for your journey. This means that wherever you may be at this point in your life, you can begin to change your course.

Roadmap

Directions for getting "unlost"—

1. **Know that you are not alone**. Whatever "lost situation" you may find yourself in, know and understand that someone else has been there before and you are not alone.

2. **Admit that you are lost and need help**. You instinctively know that you are lost, but you have to admit it to yourself and others to get the help you need. Find someone, whether it's a friend, mentor, coach, or counselor, to help you find your way. Don't get caught up thinking that you can find your way by yourself.

3. **Change lanes**. Sometimes you are just driving in the wrong lane. Get out of the fast lane. You may be creating your stress. If you are busy at work or feel that you don't have enough time for yourself, your family, or other things that you deem priorities, do your best to lighten your load. Stop taking on so many tasks at work, and at home, stop signing your kids up for all those activities. Slow down and take some things off your plate.

4. **Take the nearest exit**. Sometimes you just don't need to stay on the freeway. You may need to exit out of a job, relationship, or behavior that is not positive for you. Understand that staying on this route may lead you to a dead end.

5. **Get to the nearest rest area**. Occasionally, you need to just stop and rest. The fast pace of life and the need for urgency in accomplishing things causes unsettled spirits, sleep deprivation, and health problems. Take a break from people, technology, routines, schedules, and deadlines. Just rest!

6. **Recalculate your route**. Because you're given free will to make choices and decisions about your life, we all screw up every now and again. You were given clear directions, your internal navigation system told you where to turn, but you decided to go the opposite way—or you took a wrong turn. Like the

female GPS voice, your internal navigation system immediately detects that you did not go the way you were told and has to inform you that she is recalculating the route. What is significant to note here is that there is more than one way to reach a destination—if the road you are traveling on is too bumpy, has too much traffic, or construction, you can reroute.

7. **Make a U-turn.** If you are lost in addictive behaviors or unhealthy habits or relationships, you need to find the next street where you can make a U-turn and head in the opposite direction. Once you've discovered that you're going the wrong way, making a U-turn as soon as possible may save your life.

TWO

Time to Recalibrate

Defining Your Destiny

I N THE PREVIOUS CHAPTER, we looked at ways we get lost and people or things we may have gotten lost in. We also reflected in our journals about what ways we personally have felt lost and how we've coped with it thus far. We've decided not to be like Stubborn Sams and others who stay stuck. This is good news, because admitting that we're lost and choosing to do something about it are two necessary components to getting unlost. In this chapter we're going to look at how to recalibrate our routes so we're back on track—back on the journey to an amazing life!

First, you're going to need to make some decisions about the journey you want to make. As with any trip, it's important to start with the fundamentals: Where would you like to go? How long will it take you to get there? What route will you take? Whom are you taking with you? What are you expecting out of the journey? You may find it helpful to write down these questions in your Amazing Life notebook and leave some room for the answers. We'll take some time to think more about and answer these critical questions a little bit later, but before you begin thinking about the actual journey, you need to think about you, the driver, and about what motivates you.

The Man/Woman in the Mirror

Who Are You?

When you look in the mirror, do you have a clear indication of who is looking back at you? How much soul searching have you done to discover who you really are? I know that may sound like a strange question because after all, surely you know *yourself*. Maybe you knew your old self, but news flash—the person in the mirror is constantly changing. What you want from your life, what you enjoy doing, what scares you, etc., is not going to be the same today, as it was five or ten years ago. As humans, we are constantly growing and adapting, yet sometimes we are stuck in the mindset that we are a version of ourselves that may not fit the person we actually are now. You have changed since last year. Some of your opinions, thoughts, beliefs, likes, and dislikes have shifted. For example, I have a friend who hated sushi, and would decline every time I tried to persuade her to join me at my favorite sushi place. Apparently, she was out to lunch recently with her co-workers and they talked her into trying the "crab dynamite" roll. Her taste buds fell in love with it. Now, surprisingly enough, she's the one calling me and suggesting sushi! That's a small example, but it just goes to show you that we can always surprise others, even those who know us best. Moreover, sometimes we can even surprise ourselves.

While you must allow room for the inevitable changes in your personalities and preferences, it's also important to be in touch with what brings you satisfaction, joy, pride, and fulfillment. When you've lost touch with the core of who you are, that's when you feel lost.

That was the case for Melanie, who didn't have a clue about who she was or what she wanted from life. Reluctantly, she went to college because she wanted to please her parents. Her college days were filled with parties, hanging out with friends, and attending football games. Knowing that she eventually had to declare a major, she selected Early Childhood Education. She's not sure why she chose that, because she never liked babysitting. After graduation, instead of getting a job that followed her major, she decided to get her real estate license. That only lasted a year and she then went into retail management. Even her love of clothes didn't keep her there longer than two years. She then decided to try her skills as an actress, as she had always done well in speech and drama classes. When that didn't pan out, she became a loan officer. Although she did not really like that job, she had grown weary of job-hopping and the instability that brought. She just couldn't seem to figure out what she wanted or who she really was. Melanie was thirty-five and she still didn't have a clue.

You want to avoid falling into such a rut—or if you're already in one, you need to know how to get out. By not taking time to take a step back and figure out what she wanted from life, Melanie meandered through, always feeling discontented. Once she took the time to realize what would make her happy, she was able to take the steps she needed to achieve happiness. Through a series of tests and evaluations that she took at a career center online, Melanie discovered that she really liked to manage things and help people. She was hired on with a midsized company and has excelled in her position. At last, she found career satisfaction.

Here is a simple exercise that will help you recognize your current likes and dislikes, as well as help you discover if you're doing the things you say you like to do.

1. **Make a list of twenty things that you like.** This may include things that you like to do such as walking in the park, traveling, or reading a book. It may also include things that you like about life.
2. **Now write down twenty things that you don't like.** This could include things like spiders and spinach as well as activities like being in traffic or watching scary movies.

3. **Take a look at the list of things that you like.** How many of the things do you actually do or experience on a regular basis? If you're not experiencing the things that you say you like in life, why not? Who is stopping you from enjoying your life?

4. **Now take a look at the list of things you don't like.** Are they things that you can avoid? If there are things that you can't avoid, such as traffic, it's important to create ways to make that activity more enjoyable. For instance, listen to an informational CD, or your favorite radio station to help to alleviate the stress and dislike of the situation.

When you look at your list of likes/dislikes, is there a pattern in the list? Does the majority of your list consist of people, foods, places, or objects? It's helpful to see what your thoughts center on, because this in turn helps you identify what's important to you. If your likes were about people, then you are focused on people. If they were mainly about food, you're focused on foods, and so on.

Let's now delve deeper and explore your personal definition of success.

What Do You Want from Life?

If you were to consider your life successful, what would that look like? Success means something different to each of us. For you, it might be something like this: I want more money, I want a bigger house, I want a better job, I want a better husband, I want a better wife, I want a better car, I want a new boyfriend, I want a new girlfriend…you get the picture. But how do you define "better"? Instead of being vague, narrow in on exactly what you want. The specificity of your language dictates what you get. For example, instead of saying, "I'd like a bigger house," put a size to it, such as "I would like a 3,500-square-foot house with a swimming pool." Likewise, saying you want a better job is not definite enough; include the type of salary, benefits, travel, etc., that you would like. This sort of precision is what will bring about what you desire.

If I asked you to make a list of successful people, who would be on your list? My list would consist of Bill Gates, Oprah Winfrey, Warren Buffett, Barbara Walters, Beyoncé, and Bishop T.D. Jakes, among others. It's easy to classify these individuals as successful from what we've seen them accomplish—rising to the top of their respective fields, amassing wealth and fame along the way, and winning countless awards. On any "success list," many of the names that we recognize would be people who are "rich and famous." What about winners of the Nobel Peace Prize, which is hailed as one of the highest awards and accomplishments? Would they make your list? Think about it. As you think about that, read this next story to observe the differences of what success means to different people.

Harry and Larry were twin brothers. It was difficult for anyone to tell them apart; even their parents had trouble when they were born, and so their mother never dressed them alike. As they matured, like many twins, they took advantage of switching places and confusing people. But as much as they were alike, their fundamental definitions of success were completely different. Harry believed that his Harvard degree, seven-thousand-square-foot home with an indoor pool in a gated community, and Mercedes S-550 marked the epitome of success. Larry, on the other hand, felt that he was just as successful with his community college degree, 1,800-square-foot duplex, and five-year-old Buick. Is Harry more successful than Larry because of his material possessions? No. Larry was just as successful as Harry was because his definition of success included graduating from college with a degree, living in a small cozy house, and having no car payments or student loans bills. He accomplished his goals and reached the level he set of success.

There are certain things that some people may consider successful: finishing college, owning a home, starting a business, landing a star role in a movie/play, etc. However, what's important is what *your* version of success looks like. What does success look like for you? It is imperative that you clearly, and with as much detail as possible, define your vision of personal success. Is it having a five-bedroom home with a pool, driving a luxury vehicle, and working as an executive? Or, does your vision include owning a minivan and a three-bedroom home with a front yard? As you contemplate that question, avoid thinking about what others have accomplished or achieved. Make sure that your definition of success is about you. If you look around at other people and their so-called successes, inevitably you will begin to feel like an underachiever. There will always be someone who has more money and more ideas, and who has accomplished more goals than you. So just focus on you and the things you want.

REST STOP

Think about how you would define success. In your Amazing Life notebook, write your definition of success. It may help if you first complete these sentences.

I will be successful when I have . . .
I will be successful when I am . . .
I will be successful because I am not . . .
I will be successful because I finished . . .

Now that you know what success means to you, remember to measure yourself by *this* standard of success, not someone else's definition of success. I started my career as an educator teaching third and fourth grade. I worked in an urban school district in Oklahoma City. I had been teaching for only two years when I was tested in this philosophy. I was an innovative and vivacious teacher, and constantly worked hard to improve my skills. After attending teacher training classes given by Marva Collins, a national educator, I implemented the strategies learned at her school and had my students learning college vocabulary and Shakespeare in the fourth grade. Word got out in the district and one of the principals brought his teachers to my class to observe my classroom techniques. That afternoon, my principal called me into her office. I thought that she would be proud to have a second-year teacher who was a rising star. Instead of supporting me, she said, "Mrs. Gladney, you are good, but you are not the best, so don't get a big head." I paused for only a second and then replied, "I am the best, because I don't measure myself by anyone's standards but my own." You see, I already had defined what success meant to me. My students loved school, they loved learning, and they were above grade level, and I loved teaching. To me, that was the epitome of success.

Life-Gauging Questions

I would like for you to ask yourself three questions:

1. Am I happy with my life?
2. Am I reaching my potential?
3. Am I making a difference?

I refer to these three questions as life-gauging queries. Gauges on a car show measurements. For example, the gas gauge shows if your tank is full, half full, almost empty, etc. In order to have an amazing life, you want your happiness, potential, and make-a-difference gauges to be on "full." So think of these questions like checking the fluids and the air pressure in the tires before you hit the road. But, since this is your personal journey, and not a car trip, the levels should be *rising* rather than *declining* as you get closer and closer to your destination—your amazing life. Every few months pose these queries to yourself. If the answer is "no" to any question, or the level has dropped from your previous check-up, then you need to make some necessary adjustments to get yourself back on a course where you feel you are making the most of life.

Take some time now to reflect on the answers to these three questions and record your responses in your journal.

Set Your Mind on Success

If you live in a large city, you're probably familiar with high-occupancy vehicle lanes (HOV). These HOV lanes were developed to increase average vehicle occupancy with the goal of reducing traffic congestion and air pollution. I remember moving to Dallas and being a part of the hundreds of cars that were sitting on the freeway stuck in traffic on a regular basis. Meanwhile, there was one lane—the HOV lane—where all of the cars were driving with lightning speed. They were moving toward their destination, while those of us stuck in traffic in the other lanes watched them zoom by. To use our life journey metaphor: these people were zooming by in the "success lane," and that was enabling them to get to their destination on time. They also exercised the foresight to get in the lane in the first place by making sure they had the minimum number of passengers required and keeping alert for the limited number of entrances into the lane. They were also aware of exactly where to exit. (I have seen people try to jump into the lane at the last minute, but it's dangerous and comes with a hefty fine.) The HOV lane is for people who know where they're going and want to get there quickly. Does that sound like you? Are you prepared for success?

In order to be successful in your life, you have to make the *decision* to be successful. Decide that you want to be successful, and then act on that decision. In every area of your life that you want to make a change, you have to decide that you want to make a change. The key is in making the decision. When you commit to the decision, every fiber of your being will align itself with that decision. I'm sure you're thinking, *It can't really be that simple or everybody would be successful.* After all, you may know someone who has said they want to be successful but they're not. But saying and doing are not the same things. It's important, at this point in our discussion, to explain to you where success starts—it begins in your mind.

Let's look at Chris. He had been battling with his weight since he was in elementary school. By the time he was in high school, his doctor classified him as obese. As he grew into young adulthood, his excessive weight even got in the way of attending college. As he approached thirty he begin to realize that he may never find the girl of his dreams because it was hard for people to see beyond his weight. He had tried many diets and weight-loss plans, but they were never successful for him. Finally he reached his breaking point, and decided that he was going to lose the weight no matter what it took. His mind was made up. And, because this time was the real deal, his body began to respond. Chris lost seventy pounds that year. He looks and feels great.

To help you understand this phenomenon, I want to explain to you how the body and mind work together. First, we will take a brief look at your brain. While there are many parts to your brain, we will only focus on the two that are relevant to this chapter. The most familiar and the most talked about portion of the brain is the cerebrum, which is the largest part of the brain. It's associated with conscious thought, movement, and sensation. It consists of two halves, each controlling a side of the body. The halves are connected by the corpus callosum, which delivers messages between them. The other part that I want to emphasize is the hypothalamus, which is the master gland and is instrumental in regulating drivers and emotions. When you have a thought, it generates from your cerebrum. It's then transferred to your hypothalamus, which prompts your actions. Think of it in this way: when you make a decision, your brain tells your body to form an assembly line to get the job done. This is just another way of saying that your body aligns itself with your thoughts. If you truly want to succeed, your body will do everything possible to help you get there.

REST STOP –

Have you made up your mind? Have you decided that you truly want to change your life? If so, your body is waiting for its marching orders. It will do what is necessary to align itself in support of your decision. This requires some action steps that will be discussed in the following chapters. Your commitment to yourself begins with a signed contract. You can duplicate the writing below in your notebook, or go on to my Web site (www.creatingamazinglives.com) to download a copy.

Success Contract

I, _____, on this, the _____ day of _____, 20 _____, am making a declaration that I am in the driver's seat of my life. I am ready to take control of my thoughts, actions, and success. I have made a decision that I am ready to create an amazing life for myself. By signing this contract, I am in agreement with myself that I will do everything within my power to make a deliberate effort to be healthy in mind, body, and spirit. I understand that by doing so will result in success in every area of my life. I am truly ready to create an amazing life.

_____   _____

Signature   Date

Destiny-Defining Questions

As I mentioned before, in order to be successful, you must be very clear about what you want from life. These next three questions will help you create your own personal success system. Don't be fooled by the simplicity of the questions. It's how you answer them that will help you to determine your success. After you've looked at a question, write your answers in your Amazing Life notebook.

1. Where Am I?

This is the time to check in and find out exactly where you are on your journey. If you've ever looked at a mall directory, one of the first things you see is the big red arrow pointing to the spot that says "You are here!" Seeing exactly where you are helps you orientate yourself and know how far away you are from your destination. As I shared earlier, I had to evaluate just where I was after my twenty-year marriage ended in a divorce. I examined my life on an emotional, financial, spiritual, and physical level. I have to admit that things did not look good. When I took a hard look at where I was, I had to hold back the tears and practice my stress-breathing techniques. Nothing could have prepared me for the emotional depletion that was taking place in my body as I stared at the hard cold facts in front of me.

Perhaps you find it difficult to face your current state, but in order to move forward, you have to be prepared to confront the truth of your situation, whatever it may be. We all know people who prefer to live in a state of ignorance than acknowledge the fact that their finances or lives are in shambles. Maybe it's your brother who spends money on elec-tronic gadgets and then borrows money from you to pay his bills. Maybe your friend is in an unhealthy relationship yet claims that she's okay because she sees nothing wrong. It may be your husband who refuses to open an unpaid bill, almost convincing himself that if he doesn't look at it, the bill doesn't exist.

Behaving like Stubborn Sam will keep you stuck in a cycle of getting nowhere. Becoming "real," admitting the situation, and focusing on where you are begins recovery of any kind. To move forward in life is to have a realistic assessment of where you are.

I want you to take a minute to evaluate your life in six categories—family, job/career, finances, health, relationships, and spirituality. You can record your answers in your Amazing Life notebook.

Rate your satisfaction in these categories on a scale of 1–10 with 1 being the lowest, meaning you are not at all satisfied in this area, and 10 being the highest, meaning you are exceptionally satisfied in this area.

Family	1	2	3	4	5	6	7	8	9	10
Job/career	1	2	3	4	5	6	7	8	9	10
Finances	1	2	3	4	5	6	7	8	9	10
Health	1	2	3	4	5	6	7	8	9	10
Relationships	1	2	3	4	5	6	7	8	9	10
Spirituality	1	2	3	4	5	6	7	8	9	10

You will probably notice that your scores may be high in some areas and very low in others. The ones you scored lowest will be your priority areas for improvement. Your goal is to achieve an 8 or above in each category. Throughout the book, you will be provided with strategies that will help you increase your score in each of the categories.

---

2. Where Do I Want to Go?

Now that you have a realistic picture of how successful you do (or don't) feel in these key areas, you can begin to identify specific areas of improvement.

REST STOP

The first step in identifying what you need to improve upon is to look at the six categories again and write your desired score for each category. For example, if you rated yourself a three in the finance category, what score would you like to achieve that will make you sufficiently satisfied? Next, determine as precisely as possible why you evaluated that category with the number that you did. Perhaps you rated yourself a three because you have $15,000 in debt and only $200 in savings. Determine the dollar amount that you would need to decrease your debt by and increase your savings by that would make you satisfied and thus raise your score. Repeat this same exercise for each category that needs improvement. In the end, your chart might look something like this:

	Current score	Desired score
Family	3	10
Job/career	4	8
Finances	3	10
Health	6	9
Relationships	4	9
Spirituality	3	8

	Reason	Goal
Family	Spend only 30 minutes a day with kids	Spend at least two hours a day with them
Job/career	Feeling stagnant	Research new job opportunities
Finances	$7k debt / $200 in savings	$3.5k debt/$1,000 in savings
Health	15 pounds overweight	Lose 15 pounds
Relationships	Hardly ever check on my siblings	Commit to calling siblings 2x/month
Spirituality	Spend little time on my inner self	Spend 30 minutes a day on inspirational reading, praying, meditating

- -

3. How Do I Get There?

Gabby didn't like where things were in her life. She felt stuck at a dead-end job, had no money in savings, had a broken relationship, hadn't spoken to her sister in years, and felt like she didn't have a spiritual connection to God. So much in her life seemed broken. She knew that things needed to be fixed, but where do you start when every area of your life seems to be in shambles?

If you are like Gabby, it can feel overwhelming if more than one area of your life needs improvement. The challenge of tackling so many things may seem daunting, so you circle right back to denial and make no changes at all. The trick is to develop a blueprint for success, with goals that are small, clear, and manageable. This is where you map out the directions—the planning stage. You have to write out your goals, the plan, and a timeline. Armed with a detailed plan, you will feel more empowered to tackle changes, and feel encouraged as you check off action items.

This strategy proved to be successful for Gabby. She got back on track by first admitting that she needed help and seeking guidance. When she and I met, we created a plan for her life. We focused on one area at a time, starting on strategies for her relationships. That helped to bring a sense of peace and stability. Then she was able to focus on recovery of her finances, which included setting goals for herself such as establishing a budget, updating her résumé, and following a financial plan.

REST STOP

Let's go back and look at our finance example. In my scenario, you rated yourself a three because of high debt and low savings. And then you said you wanted to decrease it by $3,500. Is that a realistic number for you? It's time to do some number crunching. Once you have an attainable figure, you can brainstorm ways to decrease that debt to reach that goal. These ways are called action steps. One such step would be that you can cut your spending, another might be that you also need to consider ways to make additional money—a part-time job or a side business. Chapter 11 is dedicated to helping you unblock money flow and create additional income, but you can begin now to make a specific plan (your action steps) for decreasing your debt if that's in your financial category. For example, continuing with the earlier scenario, your debt is at $7,000 and you want to get down to half that plus increase your savings from $200 to $1,000. Following these four suggested steps will give you a year to meet this goal:

Step 1. Cut extra spending. Considering a family of three or four, here are some examples of things you might cut:

a. Cable—$640 yearly (opt for watching movies on DVDs that you check out for free at the library and read your news online—and watch the savings accumulate)
b. Starbucks—$440 yearly (skipping a latte twice a week adds up)
c. Eating out—$1,920 yearly (eat at home four more days a month and your family could save a bundle each year)
d. Membership/Association—fees $200 yearly (taking a break from memberships that aren't essential means more money in the bank)

You are just on step one and have already saved $3,200—that's only $300 away from the amount you wanted to pay off on your debt. To pay off your desired $3,500 and also increase your savings by $800, you still have $1,100 to go.

Step 2. Increase your monthly income (see Chapter 11 for ways to do this). To make up the remaining $1,100, you only need to make about $150 gross per month, but if you make more than that, say $450 a month (roughly an extra $100 a week), you would have almost all of your $7,000 in debt paid off as well, even with taxes and a tithe or donation to charity figured into the equation.

Step 3. As you begin to save and make money each month from these expense cuts and additional income, start paying it toward your credit card and putting some aside in savings as well so that you reach your goals in both categories by the end of the year.

Step 4. Once your debt is all paid off, continue to put aside money each month in savings so that next time an unexpected expense comes your way, you can pay in cash rather than going in debt again.

As you can see, this process is extensive, but it's imperative if you plan to make changes in your life and raise your satisfaction score. Repeat this process for each category, making goals and then action steps. By the time you finish, you will have built a systematic process for reaching all of your goals.

Setting Your Mind on Goals

I am certain that you have heard time and time again how important it is to have goals and write them down, and perhaps you are even familiar with the research around goal setting. For instance, in 1979 the Harvard School of Business interviewed new graduates from the Harvard's MBA program and found that:

- 84 percent had no specific goals at all.
- 13 percent had goals, but they weren't committed to paper.
- 3 percent had clear, written goals as well as plans to accomplish them.

In 1989, the interviewers again interviewed the graduates of that class. You can guess the results:

- The 13 percent of the class who had goals were earning, on average, twice as much as the 84 percent who had no goals at all.
- Even more staggering—the 3 percent who had clear, written goals were earning, on average, ten times as much as the other 97 percent put together.

Sociologists that have studied success and failure find that 95 percent of people never have any written goals, but of the 5 percent that do have written goals, 95 percent have reached their goals.

Despite the fact that most people would agree with the statement that setting goals is important, they don't often feel the need to take it a step further and write them down, which I believe to be vital. There are several reasons that people give for not setting or writing down goals:

1. Believe that because they know them, they don't need to write them down
2. Don't have time

3. Don't see the importance of doing it
4. Can't keep track of where they write them
5. Have no desire to do it
6. Fear of failure
7. Don't know how to write goals

To help you further understand the power of the written word and thus why it's so important to write your goals, let's take another look at how your brain works. According to studies, educational researchers suggest that approximately 83 percent of human learning occurs visually, and the remaining 17 percent comes from the other senses—11 percent through hearing; 3.5 percent through smell; 1 percent through taste; and 1.5 percent through touch. Because your brain processes information visually, it's extremely important that anything you deem important and want to remember be written down in order to stimulate your brain and to store in your memory. Simply put, you can forget what you don't see. So goal writing equals success, which means, you'll want to get started on writing your goals down right away!

Let's look at how to write specific goals. These goals are what I refer to as **TARGET** goals. TARGET is an acronym for tangible, achievable, reward, growth related, exciting, and timeline. Here's an example of a TARGET goal:

Tangible—Cleaning out the garage.
Achievable—Yes, but I may need some help from a friend.
Reward—Will treat myself to dinner for accomplishing this task.
Growth related—Doing this will help me get organized.
Exciting—I'll be able to park my car inside.
Timeline—I will do it over the weekend.

So the actual goal would be written out as follows:

Goal—I will call Tracy to help me clean out the garage this weekend to help me get organized and be able to park my car. Dinner is on me for our hard work.

You've admitted that you're lost and you've decided to get unlost. You've made a decision to change and you signed a contract with yourself. You've looked at who you are and how you're doing in six critical life categories. Now it's time to look at those fundamental questions, which were listed at the beginning of this chapter, and write down the answers to those questions in your notebook: Where you would like to go? What route will you take? How long will it take you to get there? Whom are you taking with you? What are you expecting out of the journey?

Now that you know more about the process of setting goals, you can fill in specifics for some of those questions using the TARGET approach detailed above.

Roadmap

Use these steps to help you prepare for your journey:

1. **Chart your route**. Planning and writing your goals is the only way you are going to get to your destination.
2. **Pack necessary supplies**. Gather the important things that you will need to accomplish your goals. For example, you may need to purchase large trash bags and steel shelves in order to clean and organize your garage. Or, if you want to lose weight, you may need to purchase a Zumba video for your workouts. Get whatever you need working within your budget to help you achieve your goal.
3. **Know your estimated time of arrival (ETA)**. The timeline for reaching your goals is crucial in helping you to achieve them. A timeline helps to motivate your body and mind into action.

4. **Divide the trip into practical miles.** Be realistic with your goals. If you don't have any savings and want to have $2,000 in savings, chances are that your current income isn't going to leave you with enough cash at the end of the month to save $500 a month and reach your goal in four months. However, as you cut expenses and earn additional income, you can save $167 per month and reach your goal in twelve months. In the same way, if you want to run a marathon and you aren't currently running, you don't want to start out running three or four miles at a stretch. Everything has to done in increments that build upon each other. Success comes in small steps. You take them one at a time.

5. **Integrate excitement into your journey.** Your goals need excitement. It gets boring doing the same thing repeatedly. When you're in the car on a long road trip, you may play music or listen to talk radio to add excitement. If you have children, you might play games or sing songs, or they might watch videos, read books, or draw pictures for stimulation. It's important to carry over this concept to your goals by adding some excitement to them. For example, if you're starting a new workout routine, buy some new, fun workout clothes. If you are cleaning out the garage, put your iPod on and listen to and/or dance to your favorite music.

6. **Stop at the rest stop when necessary.** Don't hesitate to take a break when you need to. Sometimes you may have to stop and regroup or set a new timeline for your goals. Make certain that your break is planned and you create a new strategy. You don't want your rest stop to become an indefinite detour.

7. **Celebrate your arrival.** When you achieve your goal, remember to reward yourself so you stay motivated. It can be a small incentive, such as an ice cream sundae or a new book, or a big reward, such as a trip. Choose something that you really want so that the reward itself is worth you reaching your goal.

THREE

The Main Road Block to Overcome

Defeating Your Insecurities

MY OLDEST DAUGHTER, Bria, is a natural-born speaker and actor. From the time that she was a toddler, people would encourage me to get her involved in commercials. She had the charm, personality, smile, and the talent. By the time she was in middle school, I was pushing her to take speech classes and join the debate team. I wanted her to compete and win trophies as I did in school to celebrate her God-given talents, so I was ecstatic when she signed up for speech competitions. When it came time for her to compete in the district-wide competition, I immediately went into my archives to find some of the prose, poetry, and dramatic interpretative pieces that I performed in my glory days. Although she didn't select anything from my archives, I encouraged her to do her best. She practiced and practiced while I coached and annoyed her.

As the competition day approached, I started to notice that Bria's confidence in her ability was beginning to diminish. The big day finally arrived, and her nerves began to take over. Although I was unable to be there because of a work obligation, she called throughout the day with updates. I knew that she was in trouble when she began to tell me how good everyone else was compared to her and she hadn't even performed yet. I kept trying to encourage her in every way that I could, but her confidence was shot and insecurity had settled in. When she gave her performance, it was filled with fear and self-doubt. She knew that she blew it. By the time she called me, through her sobs and shaking voice, she informed me that she didn't place in the top three. Her exact words were, "I am not good enough, and I will never do this again." How many times have you said that to yourself?

Hello, Insecurity

Everyone in life encounters one roadblock repeatedly: insecurity. For the past twenty years, I have flown around the country—working with companies, organizations, conferences, churches, schools, and individuals—listening to thousands of personal stories and answering many questions about life. The common thread that seems to underlie the majority of problems people face is a lack of self-esteem, which is to say feeling insecure about your worth and abilities. That is why I'm devoting an entire chapter to look at this major roadblock on your journey to an amazing life.

What Insecurity Looks Like

An insecure person lacks confidence in their own value and in their capabilities. They don't trust in themselves and they constantly fear that a present positive state is temporary, and will cause them loss or distress by "going wrong" in the future. Insecurity can creep into every part of your life:

- Relationships—*He is too good for someone like me.*
- Finances—*I'm always going to be broke.*
- Jobs—*I don't deserve that raise.*
- Physical appearance—*I hate my body.*
- Intellect—*I'm not smart enough to do that.*
- Material items—*If I drove a better car maybe people would think I'm somebody.*
- Spirituality—*I feel like God is forsaking me.*

When you look at the list, you can see how the fiber of self-doubt is housed in every corner of our lives. This roadblock is huge and stops many people from moving ahead. What can be done about this "silent killer" that sabotages relationships, jobs, self-esteem, and other pieces of your life? To answer that question, it is important to understand where it originates.

Where Insecurity Comes From

You were not born full of self-doubt and insecurity. It's a feeling that comes about as you develop. You learned how to feel and what to think about yourself based on your environment and the nurturing you received (or didn't receive) from your parents/caretakers from birth to adolescence. During various stages of your development, there is constant reinforcement—be it positive or negative—on your looks, behavior, and abilities. By the time you reach pubescence, you have developed an opinion of who you are, only to have it influenced by peers, whose opinions become a significant part of your psyche.

We all remember the middle and high school years, that awkward stage of trying to understand *who* you are and find an identity. Your parents could have done a terrific job of making you feel like a wonderful person, but if your peers belittled or shunned you, your self-esteem took a hit. Through development stages, these reinforcements began to shape what you *thought* about who you were. Some people never recover from those awkward days and carry those feelings of low self-esteem into adulthood.

I think it's important to pause here and look at the three components that make up one's overall evaluation of self: self-esteem, self-efficacy, and self-image.

Self-esteem (SE) is a person's overall evaluation or appraisal of his or her own worth. It encompasses beliefs and emotions, the positive or negative evaluation of the self.

Self-efficacy (SEF) is the measure of one's own competence to complete tasks and reach goals.

Self-image (SI) is the idea, conception, or mental image one has of oneself. It's what you think about yourself, including your strengths and weaknesses.

All three of these characterizations are meaningful and vital to your progress and a low rating in one is a form of insecurity. It is possible to be high in one area and low in another. Let's examine their interactions. Through these stories, you can see how the views of yourself interact and work with or against you.

HIGH SE AND SI—LOW SEF

Jerry has been working with BH Company for a while and has proved his value and worth. He knows that he is "the man" when it comes to looking the part, as he always makes sure that he is sharp and buttoned up. His manager offered him another position in the company that would require brand-new skills that he wasn't as familiar with. Although he was willing to learn, he questioned whether he was up for the job.

HIGH SE AND SEF—LOW SI

Betty was rated the most valuable team player at the travel agency where she worked. Whatever needed to be done, she was the woman for the job. She knew that she did excellent work and could run circles around everyone else when it came to customer service. Although she knew that everyone appreciated her, she constantly fretted about her weight. She knew people judged her as fat and lazy because she was overweight.

HIGH SEF AND SI—LOW SE

Isabelle was a classy woman who held her head high. She was well educated and very competent with her knowledge and skills in working with clients at her financial planning firm. Yet, the management team always questioned her projects and decisions. When a coveted promotion becomes available, her friend encouraged her to apply, but Isabelle felt she wouldn't be good at it, because there were so many people more qualified and talented than she.

How Low Self-Esteem Affects Your Life

Self-esteem, the category of security in ourselves that we are most familiar with, is linked to our mind, body, and spirit (MBS). Having low self-esteem negatively influences your life in a number of ways:

Depression: In many cases of depression, low self-esteem is an underlying factor. While it is certainly not the only cause, it is a great contributor. Not feeling good about *who* you are makes you feel that others around you don't value or appreciate you. Some of the emotions that are associated with low esteem include melancholy, pessimism, anxiety, fear, feeling troubled, and being despondent.

Panic attacks: People with low self-esteem and a negative view of themselves are driven by a great deal of fear, which leads to anxiety, sometimes leading to anxiety attacks. This fear can be debilitating, as it keeps them on guard and with a pessimistic view of life, anticipating the worse. It can keep them from making sound decisions. There is little ambition present or the resilience needed to recover from disappointments. Low self-esteem sometimes leads to self-loathing.

Anti-social behaviors: An insecure person is not confident in their ability to bring value; they question their competence, distrust themselves, and can fear the future. Insecurity may contribute to the development of certain behaviors such as shyness, social withdrawal, arrogance, aggression, or even bullying, in some cases.

As you can see, having low self-esteem is a detriment to living an amazing life. Not only does it bring about a flood of negative emotions and behaviors, but it also can keep you stuck in a cycle of hopelessness. Sometimes people have the ability to hide their feelings of insecurity from others or camouflage them through isolation or arrogance. You may never know they are deeply insecure. Such was the case for Brenda.

Most people who saw her considered Brenda to be a beautiful woman. She had thick, gorgeous hair; beautiful brown eyes; a dazzling smile; and a perfect size eight body. She had a bubbly personality and seemed to love being around people. All of that was displayed on the outside, but when I talked with Brenda, she was very sad and insecure. She said that while the world may think that she is beautiful, that's not what she sees or thinks when she looks in the mirror. The image looking back at her is sad and lonely. She doesn't feel like she fits in with other people. Where others see beauty, she sees flaws. To bring Brenda to a road of recovery, we had to discover where this feeling first developed and begin to erase the subconscious thoughts. We focused on her inward characteristics, her accomplishments, and the meaningful things in her life. Through a series of exercises and activities, Brenda became conscientious of her thoughts and reprogrammed her thoughts and energy to create positive affirmations of herself.

REST STOP

This exercise will help you to examine your inner beauty and begin to re-create a new perception of yourself.

1. Make a list of twenty things that you like about your personality.
2. Make a list of ten physical attributes that you like about yourself.
3. Look back at your list of strengths and proudly own them as your strengths.
4. Write down what makes you unique.
5. Complete this sentence: I am the essence of beauty because I am

   _____.

ROAD TO HIGHER SELF-ESTEEM

1. **Focus on your inner beauty.** You have a set of qualities that makes you uniquely you. Start to emphasize your inner magnificence by enhancing your strengths.
2. **Become aware of your insecurities.** Understanding what makes you feel insecure will help you to become conscious of your vulnerabilities and then negate those insecure thoughts.
3. **Don't compare yourself to others.** Celebrate your uniqueness. Whether it's physical or internal, everyone is different and you should celebrate and emphasize your greatness.
4. **Don't get caught up in wanting what others have.** While our society and media seem to fixate on certain beauty standards, it can breed an environment of discontent. Appreciate you. Work with, and own, what you have been given.
5. **A makeover may be in order.** Remember hair, skin, weight, and many other physical attributes can be enhanced. Sometimes a makeover is what is needed to get you feeling great and recognizing your outward beauty. So head to your favorite makeup counter for some new tips and products, or, if you feel like splurging, hire a stylist to help you capture a new look.
6. **Learn to love yourself.** Fall in love with yourself and who you are. People can only love you as much as you love yourself.

Security Blankets

We have all experienced moments of insecurity in our lives. Our culture places so much emphasis on material possessions that people buy things they can't afford just to look the part. It then becomes the cover that makes you feel secure, masking but not assuaging your insecurities. Take for instance, a status symbol we can all identify with—cars. There is a certain judgment that comes based upon the type of car a person drives. When you see someone driving a luxury vehicle, the assumption is that they must have the resources to afford the car, which places them at a certain status. When someone drives a clunker, the opposite is assumed.

I can remember driving my BMW 325 off the showroom floor. I was as proud as a peacock, and I loved how everyone looked at and responded to me. My husband and I had another luxury vehicle at the time as well. While it seemed that we could afford it, the BMW wasn't a wise financial decision in the long run because the high payments didn't allow for us to save as much as we should have. But it certainly made me feel and look good. As time moved on I had to sell my "baby" because my real babies and their car seats couldn't all fit in my car. Minivan, here I come. In that, too, I sought status.

A minivan was prestigious in the "mommy world" if your van had all the bells and whistles. After a while, it was time for another upgrade! A brand-new Lincoln Navigator was in order. Of course, life took an unpleasant turn and divorce happened. After which, I ended up with an older car that was a huge downgrade from the previous vehicles. It was what I could afford at the time, but what about my pride and dignity? I realized how much of my self-worth I had tied up in driving the "right" car, which is ridiculous. I kept reminding myself, *I am not my car.*

I would be willing to bet that you, too, have fallen into this trap of getting a boost in self-worth through a prestigious purchase like a car, designer handbag, or fine jewelry. It's not that these material possessions are in and of themselves a problem, but they become so when they become a barometer for your overall worth.

Here is a list of questions that will help you to determine your security blankets. Be as honest as you can when answering these questions, because it will help you clear your pathway to authenticity and confidence in yourself, and not things.

1. Can you think of a time in your past where you relied on a status symbol? What was it?
2. Have you made excuses for the type of car you drive, where you live, or what you wear?
3. Have you ever embellished your financial standing?
4. Have you ever purchased something you couldn't afford to impress others?
5. Do you feel good about the things that you have acquired?

- -

Jealousy, Insecurity's Close Cousin

Being jealous of someone is to have resentment that they have something you don't. You somehow believe them to be a rival and your competitor. Jealousy can also include the fear of being replaced by another person. This type of jealousy can creep into relationships. It's a destructive emotion that combines negative thoughts with feelings of insecurity, fear, and anxiety over an *anticipated* loss of something or someone you value.

Jealousy can present itself through a combination of emotions, such as anger, resentment, inadequacy, helplessness, and disgust. It can lead to fear of abandonment and feelings of rage. Everyone at some time or another has either felt jealous or experienced someone being jealous of them. While it is a familiar human emotion, it can be crippling and can destroy relationships.

There are different types of jealousy that are part of the human experience:

Family. Sibling rivalry is the most common type of family jealousy. This can happen when there are constant comparisons made of one sibling to another and/or there is more attention or favoritism given to one over the other. This behavior promotes the thought of a family member being your competitor or adversary.

(Continued)

Workplace jealousy. This happens when someone feels threatened by another person's abilities, appearance, status, and/or business relationships. When one person feels that they are deserving of what their colleague may have gotten—promotion, raise, project, or attention—an adversarial, and sometimes hostile, work environment may exist and can be the cause of conflict and power struggles among team members.

Romantic jealousy. This emotion can be experienced in long-term or short-term relationships. It's one of the most common types of jealousy because of the strong emotional bonds that can leave one open to potential heartbreak. If there's a perception or belief that one person is giving more attention or time to someone outside of the relationship, jealousy will bloom. Even the sight of a random attractive person may cause a normally secure partner to be concerned that they could be replaced.

Friendship jealousy. This is the form of jealousy that is felt in friendships. It stems from the same type of insecurities that are felt in other relationships: feelings of comparison, a fear of being replaced, and feelings of competition. For women, they may feel replaced (or that they will be replaced) by another female friend or by a new boyfriend if their friend starts to date. The same applies to men.

If you understand that jealousy stems from insecurity, then you can work toward building your confidence, which will help you rid your mind and spirit of jealousy.

Kick Up the Confidence

Now let's examine how to overcome and manage insecurity. We do this by looking at its opposite trait: confidence. Confidence is believing in yourself, your powers, and/or abilities. Self-confident people are assertive, optimistic, eager, independent, trustworthy, and have the ability to handle criticism and accurately assess their capabilities. Self-confidence is like money—we all think that everyone else has more of it than we do. In reality, it's rarely something that comes naturally or without any effort.

The effort that you put in to building your self-confidence will be worth it to help you get where you want to in life. In fact, self-confidence is one of the key ingredients to your success. Without it, it's virtually impossible to accomplish your goals. We established in the previous chapter that you cannot be successful without establishing goals. In turn, you have to believe in your ability and power to achieve your goals. However, having self-confidence does not mean that you will always succeed in what you do. If you examine the record of accomplishment of every successful person, you will find that they failed more often than they succeeded. However, they never dwelled on their failures. They concentrated on their goals, believed in themselves, and pushed ahead. Trusting in your abilities gives you a general sense of control in your life, and you believe, within reason, that you will be able to do what you wish, plan, and expect.

Your definition of success has to include a high level of confidence because it requires you to be willing to risk the disapproval of others because you trust and believe in your abilities. Since you can accept your own definition of success, you don't feel the need to conform to what others think in order to be accepted.

Self-confidence is a state of mind developed and perfected by the most successful people in the world. It's something you can create and perfect just like anyone else. Self-confidence is an attitude, which allows individuals to have positive yet realistic views of themselves and their situations. If you seriously want to create self-confidence, then you need to change the way your mind focuses on things. You need to teach yourself to create a new way of thinking and develop what I call "success energy." How many times have you seen or met someone for the first time and just gotten the sense that they are successful? You might not have exchanged a word with them but you just sense that they are a success. You're picking up what I call "success energy." You can have the same! Yes, you can. Self-confidence is not given to you; it's created. This means that you can create self-confidence to any degree you want.

It's list time. This exercise will help you to examine many of the "greats" in your life and acknowledge the successes you've had. Making lists, rereading them, and rewriting them from time to time will help build your self-confidence.

Make a list of . . .

1. **At least five things you admire about yourself.** Examples include the way you've raised your children; the good relationship you have with your brother; or your strong spirituality.

2. **The five greatest achievements in your life so far.** This could include recovering from a serious illness; graduating from high school; or learning to use a computer.

3. **At least twenty accomplishments (small or large).** These accomplishments can range from simple, like learning to cook or going to the gym faithfully, to advanced, like getting a post-graduate degree.

4. **Ten ways you can "treat" or reward yourself.** This list should not include food or items with a price tag. Think of walking through a park, napping, watching your children playing on a playground, or catching up with a friend.

5. **Ten things you can do to make yourself laugh.** This can be anything from watching your favorite comedy to trying on silly hats.

6. **Ten things you could do to help someone else.** These things can range from something small like baking cookies for a sick friend or mowing an elderly neighbor's yard to something more involved like dropping dinner off at your busy sister's house or cleaning out your parent's basement.

7. **Ten things that you do that make you feel good about being yourself.** Examples could include being a good mom, running in a 5K, or having a green thumb.

How did you do? Did you struggle to complete any of the lists? If you did, that helps you identify the area(s) that you need to work on. For instance, if you had difficulty identifying twenty accomplishments over your lifetime, this could indicate that you don't feel good about things that you've done, or that you don't view them as praiseworthy. When you are able to complete that (troublesome) list, look over it and feel proud about the things that you've done. You may feel or have been taught to feel that you shouldn't focus on or talk about your accomplishments, because that's being conceited or being a show-off. However, when you can focus your energy on your positive behaviors, your perspective of yourself is enhanced. I have dealt with many people who shun themselves, diminish their accomplishments, and/or don't reward themselves, and end up feeling inadequate and unhappy. To overcome this, continue to add to these lists. Look over them, think about them, and study them. Work on believing the great things about yourself that you have listed. It will really help to kick your confidence into gear.

Roadmap

Boosting your self-confidence.

1. **Think positively about yourself.** Refer back to your list and your positive traits, strengths, and things that you admire about yourself.
2. **Set goals that are realistic and will meet your expectations.** For instance, set your goals at a reasonable level so that what you accomplish is equal (or almost equal) to what you set out to accomplish. This can boost your self-confidence and self-satisfaction.

3. **Reward/praise yourself when you have done well.**
4. **Whenever something upsetting or disappointing occurs, be aware of your thoughts.** Think logically about the situation instead of reacting merely on the basis of your emotions.
5. **Focus on your strengths.** Don't dwell on your weaknesses.
6. **Realize that there are certain things that you are more adept and competent in than others.** Acknowledge that it's impossible to expect perfection in every aspect of your life.
7. **Do not attribute your achievements and accomplishments only to luck.** Instead, give yourself credit for achievements that have come as a result of your effort and hard work.
8. **Learn to be assertive.** That is, learn to express your feelings, opinions, beliefs, and needs directly, openly, and honestly, while not violating the rights of others. For example, learn to stand up for your rights and say "no" to unreasonable requests.

FOUR

Deciding to Go Off-Course
Facing—and Overcoming—Your Fears

E RICA LOVED WRITING. From the time that she understood how to put together a sentence, she started writing short stories. Her teachers constantly praised her for her excellent writing skills and her creative ideas. She even worked as one of the editors for the online papers of her high school and college. Unfortunately, her parents viewed writing as more of a hobby than a career, so she majored in marketing. Although she thrived as a marketing representative, Erica couldn't shake the desire to become a writer. But, every time she thought of pursuing her passion, her fears, doubts, and financial worries would overtake her. Caring for her mother and her current job requirements also didn't leave much free time to start writing. So, she decided that it would never work and that it was time to retire her pen.

What Are You Afraid Of?

How many times has fear stopped you in your tracks? Fear can be a powerful and paralyzing emotion. When we're presented with danger, our natural reaction is to respond with fear. I call that "real" fear, which means it's related to a tangible threat to your safety or well-being. Real fear is actually helpful because it alerts you to danger and helps your body decide how to respond. When you're afraid, your response is either to run from the danger, or fight it. The other type of fear, and one that is far more common, is what I call "imagined" fear and that pertains to feelings of acute anxiety and panic when it comes to dealing with situations that place us outside of our comfort zones but don't actually pose any physical danger. Both types of fear have real and sometimes lasting consequences on our thoughts, behavior, and ultimately, how you live your life.

In this chapter, we'll examine the power of fear, both real and imagined. We'll also explore the different types of fears that hamper your success. And, you'll be given strategies that will help you to manage and overcome your fears.

Real Fear

Many events can happen to us in life wherein we experience true fear. I have worked with many clients who have experienced unimaginable trauma, such as incest, rape, accidents, illness, abuse, abandonment, abduction, and stalking. Experiences like these can take on a life of their own causing the victim to feel a pervasive sense of anxiety, mistrust, and insecurity long after the stressful event. I can attest to this personally as I experienced a harrowing event in my childhood that enveloped me in fear at a very early age.

I can remember it like it was yesterday. I was in the fifth grade, and I usually walked with my neighbors to the bus stop. But, because they weren't ready, I continued on my own so that I wouldn't miss my bus. I had almost reached the bus stop when a man jumped in front of me holding a broken glass bottle. Terrified, I screamed for help, but he started choking me and carried me into his garage where he put me in a corner amid lawn mowers and junk. I could smell the stench of dirt, oil, and rust as I prayed to God for help. Suddenly, he came at me with a knife, placing it to my throat, while spitting the venomous threat, "I will kill you if you make another sound." I remember begging, "Please let me see my family again." He screamed and shouted, "SHUT UP! I already raped a girl and I will kill." I had heard about the rape a couple of weeks earlier.

He explained that his plan was to keep me there until my sixth-grade neighbor walked by. He planned to grab her and rape her, because she was more developed than me. It seemed like an eternity as I stood there shaking with fear. I eventually began to hear voices of people nearby. Suddenly the man shouted "Get out of here!" and I ran with super-human strength into the arms of the people whose voices I had heard who were gathering at the corner. I knew that God had heard my prayers since I escaped without physical harm.

As you can imagine, I never made it to school that day. My safe world had been shattered and I became full of a life-altering fear. As an eleven-year-old, I had trouble processing what had happened to me, and I began to experience terrible nightmares and panic attacks. Like so many others, I wasn't put into counseling, as I should have been, but over time, I developed my own coping skills, which helped me to overcome my fear of being alone, walking by myself, and even trusting others.

Many of you reading these pages have also experienced a traumatic event at one point in your life and you may still be dealing with the effects, which could include panic attacks, anxiety, nightmares, paranoia, depression, etc.... I urge you to get professional counseling. Below I have listed some strategies that will help you to manage fear that may have resulted from your experience.

ROAD TO RECOVERY FROM REAL FEAR

1. **If this event was uncontrollable, understand that it wasn't your fault.** When these types of incidents occur, it's common to blame yourself, and start down the road of could'ves, should'ves, and would'ves. Processing these occurrences as if somehow there was something you could have done helps you to maintain some type of control of the situation. When you feel or think that you have no control, you feel open and vulnerable. Blaming yourself only blocks your healing. Remember: *it was not your fault.*

2. **Remember, if you can survive it, you can revive from it.** You will never truly understand why any random act of violence happens. The sad fact of human existence is that evil exists and sometimes it touches us and we can't avoid it. You may be inclined to think that you somehow deserved it, but you did NOT deserve it. You have it within you to not only get through any experience but become empowered, stronger, and more resilient as a result.

3. **Declare power over the fear.** This means that you make the decision that you will not let the event, person, or experience dominate your life by controlling your thoughts and emotions.

4. **Write down any learned lessons.** As difficult as it may be, write down the lessons from your particular experience. This will help you draw strength from the experience.

5. **Seek professional counseling.** Counseling is always advisable as it helps you talk through the experience and move toward healing.

False Fear

Fear is, of course, a very real and genuine emotion, but often what we fear is imagined or unfounded, and this can hold you back in life. Think of imagined fear as the acronym F.E.A.R., which stands for *False Evidence Appearing Real*. Imagined fears can take many forms, and they can undermine your ability to live the amazing life you desire. Imagined fear is what prevented Erica, mentioned at the beginning of the chapter, from following her dreams of becoming a writer. A few common imagined fears include:

- Fear of failure
- Fear of success
- Fear of loss
- Fear of what others think

- Fear of others
- Fear of one's self

Let's look at each type of fear, what it means, and how it can hinder your success.

FEAR OF FAILURE

Fear of failure is the distressing emotion that whatever you try or do, you will be unsuccessful. Because you're afraid of not reaching your goals, you don't even try. For some people, failure is seen as something negative that should be avoided at all costs, instead of an experience that you can learn from (and one that is inevitable). This fear keeps people constantly running away from hard work, dreams, relationships, and effort. This type of fear is the most common, and if you are honest with yourself, I am certain that at some time in your life you have experienced this feeling.

FEAR OF SUCCESS

Fear of success means that you feel anxiety thinking about how your efforts might lead to great success. It seems counterintuitive, but it's nonetheless a very real fear for some who fear that success will disrupt their lives and bring about changes in normalcy, lifestyle, structure, and even their personality. For example, you could fear losing weight and becoming more attractive because of how it may affect your current relationship. Or you may fear getting the big promotion at work, because there may be more demanding hours that will keep you away from the family. Indeed, we have all witnessed how fame and financial success can negatively affect people's family dynamics and friendships or how it can lead to self-destructive behaviors, and you may fear going down one of these paths. In all of these scenarios, you cling to your safe place and you, consciously or not, put barriers in place to keep from succeeding.

FEAR OF LOSS/ABANDONMENT

Fear of abandonment is felt when someone you love has gone away, be it through divorce, death, or a personal decision to disconnect from your life. This typically happens in childhood and the feelings are carried into adulthood and manifest as believing that those that love you will leave you. The fear of loss is similar to the fear of abandonment. It's the crippling worry that someone or something will always disappear from you. It may be that you fear losing your job, house, car, savings, parents, kids, friends, health, or something else. Because this fear is so paralyzing, you irrationally cling to people or things, which can lead to disorders like hoarding. Or, conversely, you avoid emotional connection all together so as to avoid losing something or someone you love or value.

FEAR OF WHAT OTHERS THINK

Fear of what others think is a debilitating preoccupation with what others may or may not be thinking and saying about you. Through this you become motivated to seek the approval of other people. This type of fear can drive you to buy things you can't afford, dress a certain way, live a certain way, and become someone you don't recognize. On the other hand, fear of disapproval can stop you from trying new things, being authentic, and speaking your mind. If we are all honest, we have all found ourselves, at some point, caring too much about what somebody else thinks of us. What is interesting about this fear is that most of the time you don't really know what *they're* thinking, so it's what you *think* they are thinking. Think about that for a minute!

FEAR OF ONE'S SELF

Fear of one's self is the feeling of being afraid of who you really are. Wow! That should strike a chord for some people. Yes, some people really are running from themselves. What does that mean? You avoid examining yourself introspectively because of what you may find. You find that you live in denial of your strengths or weaknesses for fear that you may not like who you really are. It takes strength and maturity to understand and embrace your true self.

This became so profound to me after having a conversation with my absentee father. As an adult, I sat down and had a conversation with him to try to understand why he left his family before I was born. The more I found out about him and his past, the more I realized that I was a lot like him. How could that be? He was an alcoholic, a "ladies" man, and a dead-beat dad, who was obstinate, skeptical, and incredibly selfish. I was nothing like that! But he was also entrepreneurial, creative, tenacious, bold, and unafraid of others. I had to be honest with myself and acknowledge that I was like him in some ways. There were several traits of his that I had, both good and bad.

ROAD TO RECOVERY FROM IMAGINED FEAR

1. **Recognize and acknowledge that the fear is just your imagination.** Think back to when you were a kid and had an imaginary friend, or when you played "pretend." Well, I had a pretend classroom and I was a pretend teacher. My students were rocks and they had names. My classroom was beautiful, well you get the picture. My imagination allowed it to be anything that I wanted. That is what is happening with your fear. Your imagination is painting a picture of something only you could see.

2. **Ask yourself these questions:**
   a) Where does this fear come from?
   b) What experiences have I had that make me believe this is real?

3. **Refocus your imagination and "pretend" that you are not afraid.** The same way that you convince yourself that something is real is the same way you convince yourself that it is false. Your subconscious will internalize that it is false and respond accordingly.

4. **Practice to work out your fears**. Some fear-buster methods encourage you to confront your fears head on—whatever you are afraid of, put yourself in that situation. While I would not encourage that without the proper guidance, you can practice techniques to help you work out the fears. Through this you're harnessing and focusing your energy on building up power and strength rather than using your energy on being fearful. For instance, if you're afraid to speak in public, you might not want to start out speaking in front of a large group of people (facing the fear head on), but you could sign up for a class on public speaking and practice. By doing this, you build your confidence and become less and less fearful. As you build confidence in yourself and your abilities, you will increase your self-esteem and your self-efficacy.

5. **Increase your knowledge**. Fear is great when knowledge is small. Learn more about what you are afraid of. If it's flying, you should study planes; if it's spiders, then learn about their value; if it's finances, learn more about numbers.

Be Like Mike

When trying to overcome fear, it's helpful to research some of your favorite successful people or role models and explore how they overcame their fears. I am constantly motivated by the success of others who have overcome their fears and accomplished their dreams.

One of my heroes is Michael Jordan. I was awed by his talent but even more fascinated with his story of being cut from the high school basketball team and overcoming his fears to become one of the greatest basketball players of all time. This is what he had to say about overcoming his fears: "I've missed more than 9,000 shots in my career. I've lost almost three hundred games. Twenty-six times I've been trusted to take the game-winning shot and missed. I've failed over and over and over again in my life. And that is why I succeed."

REST STOP

Which one or more of the fear categories—fear of failure, fear of success, fear of loss, fear of what others think, and fear of one's self— are holding you hostage, keeping you from exploring your dreams, expanding your mind, and achieving your potential? In order to release and manage fear, you have to know what it is that you fear. Look at these five fears and identify which type of fear(s) that you have. In your notebook, make a list of additional fears you may have that I did not list.

Fears

1.

2.

3.

4.

5.

Now beside your list, I want you to write, if it is real or imagined. If it is a real fear, such as what I experienced in the story that I told earlier, review the management techniques that I shared to help you work through that (Road to Recovery from Real Fear). If your fears are imagined or false, practice the strategies I reveal in Road to Recovery from Imagined Fear.

Facing and overcoming your fears will not happen overnight. Like everything else that we discuss in this book, it takes making a conscious effort and takes time. Allow yourself the necessary time to defeat the subconscious thoughts.

Roadmap

Banishing fear from your life.

1. **Acknowledge that your fears exist.** The first step to over-coming, conquering, and defeating anything is to acknowledge that it exists in your life. Once you do that, it empowers you to confront the fear, real or imagined.

2. **Don't let fear keep you on the wrong course.** If you are living your life and it doesn't look how you want it to, don't let fear keep you miserable and unhappy. Work through your fears using the tips and strategies I suggested earlier so you can get on the right course for you.

3. **Don't let fear take you off the right course.** Sometimes you are doing what you should be, but then because of your fears of success, failure, or what others think, you can find yourself wandering to a different course that is not right for you. Again, face that fear head on.

4. **Make your own decisions for your life.** Don't allow fear of others—what they say, do, or think—to determine what you say, do, or think. Millions are living their life based on other people. If you find yourself often saying or thinking, *I don't want them to think*…then there is a strong chance that you are allowing others to dictate your actions. Don't be guilty of keeping up with the Joneses.

5. **Know that you have the power over fear.** You really have to believe in your heart that you have power over fear. The emotion of fear is so strong and gripping that it can trick you into believing that you have no power. That is not true. You are in the driver's seat of your life and you get to decide how to respond to all of your experiences. Choose power. Repeat to yourself, "I am not afraid of _____."

6. **Become spiritually connected.** Being spiritually connected to a higher power helps you to understand that there is a presence that is bigger and stronger than yourself that can protect and defend you. As I shared in my story earlier about being abducted, I said a prayer and felt God's presence there. He protected me from further harm and danger.

7. **Seek professional help.** Some real fears may require the need for counseling. A good counselor can help you to pick up pieces and give you a different perspective on things.

FIVE

The Detour: You *Thought* It Made You Late

Dealing with Your Thoughts and Beliefs

YOU SET YOUR ALARM for 6:15 a.m. this morning, but when the buzzer went off, you hit the snooze button a couple of times to get a few extra minutes of precious sleep. You're finally awake, but running a few minutes late. You rush around, figuring you can make that up on the road. You grab yogurt and a banana for breakfast and scurry out of the door. You had planned to review the agenda for this morning's meeting, but in your haste, you left it on the counter. Things are moving along smoothly and then a big detour sign appears. As luck would have it, a construction project has started, which means you'll have to take the longer, alternate route around town. Meanwhile, the clock keeps ticking. You arrive ten minutes late and the meeting has already begun. Thoroughly embarrassed, you apologize explaining that a *detour* made you late.

I'm sure we have all experienced a scenario similar to the one detailed above. Let's analyze it for a moment. Your day started out behind schedule, because you *decided* to sleep an extra twenty minutes, which threw your schedule off for the morning. Because you were in a hurry, you didn't have time for your energizing mental morning exercise; you didn't have time to stop and eat breakfast; and you forgot the meeting agenda on the counter. You *thought* that you would drive a little faster to work to make up the difference, and then there was a detour. You immediately thought, *If it wasn't for that detour I wouldn't have been late.* However, there was a detour, and your lateness was entirely your fault.

Our Thoughts Direct Us

Many of your thoughts can keep you from taking responsibility for your actions. Although many people have talked and written about thoughts through the years, in this chapter I am going to help you actually *see* your thoughts and process them in a different way. I once heard the statement, "Where you are in life is a direct reflection of where you *thought* you would be." You might be thinking, *How could that be? I didn't want to be in the midst of bankruptcy; laid off; divorced; broken; wild kids; pregnant; in a toxic relationship; depressed; sick; etc. Do you really mean to tell me that I thought my way here?* Before you completely shut down, or think that I am kicking you while you're down, continue reading this chapter and you'll be enlightened. I'm not telling you "bad news." It's actually great news, because it means that you can reformulate your thoughts and your life! Keep reading, you'll see.

According to the National Science Foundation, you have about 50,000 to 60,000 thoughts running through your mind each day. While that's hard to comprehend, many of these thoughts are subconscious, fleeting, and minuscule. Moreover, many of our thoughts are consumed with the past; mistakes that were made; battling guilt; planning for the future; or just daydreaming. The sad part is that some researchers have estimated that 70 to 80 percent of the thoughts that we have are negative or neutral. That is huge! That means that there are really only a small percentage of your thoughts that are positive, meaningful, and productive.

Let's look at this another way to help you visualize what's happening. Let's assume, as the saying goes, you get a penny for your thoughts. If that's the case—translating your thoughts into money—you can collect 60,000 pennies a day, which equals $600 a day. If you take the $600 and multiply it by 365 days, you would make $219,000 a year from your thoughts. Now assuming, as research has suggested, that 80 percent of your thoughts are negative and nonproductive, we will subtract 80 percent from the total, which leaves you with $43,800.

Mathematical Positive Thought Formula
Potential – 100% or $219,000
60,000 thoughts/100 pennies = $600 a day × 365 days a year
= $219,000
Actual – 20% or $ 43,800
12,000/100 = 120 × 365 = $43,800
Amount you're missing out on – 80% or $175,200
$219,000
− $43,800
$175,200

What this illustrates is that your thought potential could be worth almost a quarter of a million dollars per year, but because you don't control them or focus on positivity and productivity, they are worth only $43,800 a year. That's a $175,200 difference. Imagine the difference that an extra $175,200 could make in your life right now.

So look at this formula from a psychological point of view. If you could turn the negative thoughts into positive ones, you could increase the positive impact on your life by the equivalent of $175,200. If you controlled your thoughts and redirected them to their positive potential, your life would begin to expand exponentially. Again, you are in the driver's seat and have total control of your thoughts, so the question then becomes, what is on your mind? Are your thoughts killing your dreams or are they propelling you to success?

To understand how you can start to change your thoughts and actions, it's important to review how the mind actually works. While some of this information may not be new to you, allow me to do a review so that you can really see your thoughts.

A Penny for Your Thoughts

To help you become more aware of your thoughts, get a jar, cup, or container, and keep a handful of pennies handy. Pennies are in abundance so you can keep them in your car, at your desk, pocket, purse, etc. For one week, each time you have a positive thought drop a penny in your cup. Count the pennies at the end of the week to see how positive your thoughts have been.

Controlling Your Intentional Thinking and Hidden Beliefs

Instead of using the same old terminology, I want you to *see* this differently. I will alternate between "conscious" for intentional and "subconscious" for hidden. I will use the analogy of the car to help explain the conscious and the subconscious mind concept. The car's body, interior, buttons, and gadgets are all components that you can touch, adjust, push, and pull with intentional and deliberate certainty. When you turn the ignition, the car starts and you are ready to go. Similarly, the deliberate part of your mind (conscious) is responsible for your awareness, analytical thinking, problem solving, and cognitive learning. These processes happen very deliberately.

The hidden part of the car is where the operations and programming of the vehicle takes place. You are unaware of the inner workings of the engine, carburetor, alternator, battery, etc. Thousands of parts and programming codes are working to make sure that your car works when you turn it on. If one small part is out of alignment, your car can be thrown off balance and won't be able to function properly. Although these parts are *hidden*, they work automatically, when we *intentionally* insert the key or push a button. The hidden part of our mind (subconscious)—similar to a car's operating system—is vital and substantial. Most of the millions of pieces of information that you deal with every second crosses into this vast space. Your subconscious is in charge of your emotions, memories, core beliefs, and values. While it stores your memories, it can also close off and suppress traumatic events you may not be ready to deal with. It's also responsible for all physiological functions of the body: heart rate, breathing, organ operation, blinking, etc. While the subconscious is in control of all of our automatic movements, we are unaware of this happening in our intentional (conscious) mind.

Assigning Value to Your Thoughts

Now that we have a basic understanding of how these two components of the mind operate, we will investigate how to put the power of this subconscious to use when it comes to taming your thoughts. It's critical that you understand that you are a reflection of the thoughts that are stored in your subconscious. Since your emotions, values, and beliefs are all stored in your subconscious, the work you need to do to reformulate your thoughts begins there. Because the subconscious is so powerful, it can dominate you and play tricks on you. Just as one misplaced spark plug in the engine can keep your car from moving forward, one wrong thought in your mind can keep your life from moving forward.

Look at this scenario. You have convinced yourself (subconsciously) that your colleague Linda wants your job. Every time you see her talking to someone, you believe that she's talking about you and is plotting with other co-workers to undermine your position. Now everyone seems to act "funny" toward you at work. You can't get your work done because you're thinking about the betrayal that you've convinced yourself will soon take place. These thoughts start to affect your attitude and productivity. When your boss calls you in her office to talk to you about your productivity and your effectiveness, you don't hear anything she says because you're thinking about Linda, who you think is behind all of this.

More than likely, your boss isn't aware of your concerns, but she has just been watching and evaluating your productivity, which has been affected by your thoughts of Linda. So in the end, Linda was the reason that you were called into the office, but not in the way you thought. While your initial thought, or feeling, may have been true—*Linda wants your job*—you assigned value to that thought, meaning you let yourself believe that it was valid and important. Since every thought manifests itself in some way or the other, you chose to act on the thought instead of dismissing it. I'm sure there are many scenarios that you can replace with the one that I just illustrated. Think of how many times that you have let your thoughts run amuck and your imagination has taken over. When your imagination and logic are in conflict, your imagination invariably takes the lead.

Yes, your thoughts are *that* potent.

Thinking Your Way into—and out of—a Rut

If you've ever said to yourself, "Things just don't seem to work out for me," or "I can't seem to get a break," you've just thought and behaved your way into a rut. Your actions follow your thoughts, so you will unconsciously make sure that things don't work out for you. Let me give you an example.

For most of my life, I have been a driven person. I have always believed that I could achieve my goals and make things happen. When I moved to different city and had to start from square one, I began to feel that I just couldn't get a break. I thought it, spoke it, lost my drive, and behaved my way right into stagnation. It was hard for me to break loose from the cycle of thinking that it just wasn't "my time," or this was just a season in life when I wasn't supposed to experience success.

It wasn't until I changed my thoughts about my situation that I begin to experience some positive change. In essence, I modified my life by changing my thoughts and feelings, which in turn caused me to behave differently. Instead of waiting for a break, I created my own opportunities. It was amazing how things began to fall into place, because I changed my mind and stopped being my own worst enemy.

You Think You Can

When I was in elementary school, the popular children's book *The Little Engine That Could* was required reading. Since then, I have doubted myself numerous times, but when I think about those words, *I think I can, I think I can, I think I can*—which is what the little engine said so it could get over the big hill—I am inspired to keep trying. I really believe that this early programming of my mind had something to do with the fact I earned a doctorate degree years later. At the time that I was graduating with my master's degree, I had two babies, ages one and two, with one on the way; I was running my own business; and I had just started a nonprofit organization for teenage girls. Right before graduation, one of my advisers encouraged me to apply to Oklahoma University's doctoral program. He offered to extend my existing academic scholarship to pay for the program, which would involve two additional years of coursework and another year for the dissertation.

My immediate thoughts came barreling from my subconscious, *This is crazy! Don't even think about it! You're getting ready to have child number three; you need to focus on what you have already. Why do you need a doctorate? What will people think? You have children you need to pay attention to. Three more years of school is a long time. You have already gone to college for seven years; aren't you smart enough?*

Well fortunately, I knew how to conquer the thoughts in the conscious space where I could stop and think logically. My conscious thoughts went something like this: *You are already in the flow of school. You don't have to take a break, just keep moving. It's only four semesters. You'll be done in no time. You can't turn down a free education. You are valued here. Dr. Gladney has a nice ring to it. I think I can, I think I can.*

I had to reprogram my brain and use strategies to conquer negative thoughts. I used these same techniques to constantly keep myself focused and filled with positive thoughts throughout the program, especially when things became challenging. There were times when I did want to quit, but I kept going. It was a triumphant moment for me as I stood up on the stage to receive my graduation hood, thinking, *I knew I could, I knew I could, I knew I could.*

Is it possible to think your way to greatness? Absolutely! Think of the many successful people that you've heard talk about their success during an interview. It doesn't matter if they are in sports, entertainment, or business, they all will say how they envisioned their success (thought it), rejected naysayers (dismissed negative energy), and created their own rituals, affirmations, and positive reinforcements (conquering their thoughts) to get to their greatness.

Your thoughts are very powerful—let them be tools for your success, not weapons against it. As you take time to examine your thoughts, I would like to mention one of my favorite poems, *Thinking* by Walter Winter. I am sure you have heard it quoted. It begins with, "If you think you are beaten, you are." Again, your thoughts control your outcome.

ROAD TO DELIBERATE POSITIVE THINKING

1. **Acknowledge that your thoughts are potent and carry energy.** Your thoughts, whether positive or negative, are filling your body with some type of energy. Positive thoughts breed positive feelings and negative thoughts breed negative feelings.
2. **Become aware of your thoughts.** Start to be in a conscious state of mind and be intentional about what your mind is processing so that you can catch yourself and redirect thoughts as needed.
3. **Block negative thoughts with positive ones.** When you catch a negative thought, turn it into something positive. For instance, when you have a negative thought about your co-worker, also think about how great it is to have a job.

Thought Energy and Four of the Energy Bodies

Your thoughts not only dictate your actions, but they also carry energy. How does that work? Taking a further look at how your body is made may help you understand. As with everything else in the atmosphere, our bodies are made up of energy. Another way to think of your body is that it is a field full of unseen signals. It's constantly sending out waves and signals that most often can't be touched or felt. Diseases, illnesses, injuries, and mental and physical problems are all caused in part by disturbances in energy fields. Conversely, diseases, illnesses, and other physical and mental problems will rapidly improve once the disturbances are removed and the specific disturbed fields are restored. Research by scientist Barbara Brennan indicates that there are between five and nine bodies of energy. It's important that all of your energy bodies are in alignment to create success and harmony in mind, body, and spirit. Understanding how this works should also help you see the ways that you can positively and negatively impact yourself, as well as others. This philosophy has been referred to as a number of things: law of attraction; boomerang theory; karma; or biblically stated, "You reap, what you sow." Whichever way you prefer to say it, it all means the same thing. What you do, say, and how you act is going to come back to you the same way. Understanding the bodies of energy will also help you know how to keep your health in balance.

For simplicity sake, we will only discuss four of the energy bodies: the physical, the emotional, the mental, and the spiritual.

The Physical Energy Body

The Physical Energy Body is the most commonly known energy body. Our physical bodies are made up of atoms, molecules, and cells. These are all forms of vibrating energy that we have traditionally called "matter." It is in this body of energy that we experience the senses of touch, taste, and smell.

The Emotional Energy Body

The Emotional Energy Body contains the emotional patterns, feelings, and vibrations that determine our personality, and also how we feel about ourselves and interact with others. If we are constantly angry, always feel helpless, or are consistently fearful, these patterns or vibrations get locked in our emotional energy field and become a part of our personality. This determines, to a very large degree, how we interact with others on personal, social, and cultural levels.

The Mental Energy Body

The Mental Energy Body contains your thoughts and belief systems. There is a very strong connection between the mental and emotional bodies. Even though a thought or idea can itself be very powerful, your reactions to those thoughts carry even *more* energy. For example, take the thought that *the only way to get a quality education is to attend a private school.* One person might hear that thought or idea, and think that it was silly, and give it absolutely no energy. But another person might become very passionate about it—depending on his/her greater belief systems—and argue strongly for or against the truth of that statement. His/her emotional body would then record the intensity of the reaction to the thought stored in the mental body. However, the person who thought the statement was silly in the first place would not have any resonance with it, and no energetic pattern would be stored in either the mental or emotional bodies.

The Spiritual Energy Body

The Spiritual Energy Body contains all the information related to our experiences and reflects our consciousness of all that has been learned and experienced. It contains our higher intentions; our sense of what is right and wrong ("conscience"); and our desires to increase our awareness of our purpose, place, and mission for this lifetime.

A Journey into the Physical and Mental Energy Bodies

If this has been your first introduction to energy bodies, it may sound unfamiliar and curious to you. It used to be unfamiliar to me as well, and then I experienced firsthand its importance in terms of good health. My middle daughter became ill at the age of six, which led us on a seven-year journey. It all started when she came down with strep throat that lasted for six weeks. During that time, she was prescribed three different types of antibiotics. A few weeks later, she began to complain of severe stomach pains, which she described as something moving around in her stomach. Although there was no diagnosis, she was given medicine for gastritis. Soon after, she started complaining about pain in her hip and having problems walking. That, coupled with a fever and pain, prompted us to take her to the emergency room. After several hours of testing, she was rushed via ambulance to Children's Medical Center and was diagnosed with *septic hip*, a bacterial infection which lodges in the hip and can cause permanent damage if not removed. The doctors performed an emergency surgery that was successful; however, it didn't stop her stomach pains. We then took her to a specialist who diagnosed her with "abdominal migraines." Again, another diagnosis that I hadn't heard of that we treated with medication.

A few weeks later she developed severe dizziness. Her equilibrium was compromised, which in turn affected her balance. This sickness required another emergency room visit. They admitted her to Children's Medical Center again, where she spent six days. Doctors administered several tests, two spinal taps, and several rounds of different types of medications; she was diagnosed with atypical migraines and released. However, the medication that was prescribed for her still didn't work.

Having exhausted all traditional methods and specialists, we took her to see an allergist. After going through a series of tests, the allergist informed us that the antibiotics she had taken two years earlier had actually stripped the lining of her intestines. This had killed off the good antibodies, which had previously protected her from the food she was allergic to, and it was now able to poison her system. We began nontraditional treatments and a thirty-day detox. She was put on a strict diet, which included several supplements.

She felt good for the next year, but then the sickness hit her body again. This time taking a different form. She was unable to hold down food or water for multiple days at a time. Her body rejected anything that touched her mouth. Her new diagnosis was "cyclical vomiting syndrome," which was another disease we had never heard of. Of course, this required hospital stays since she had to be fed intravenously. We were informed that there was no known cause for the disease, nor was there a treatment. We would just have to let it run its course each time it flared up. All of these experiences for her added up to seventy-plus missed days of school; five spinal taps; more than fifteen ER visits; five hospital stays; seven specialist appointments; one surgery; four outpatient procedures; ten different diagnoses; and tons of prescriptions. I finally took her to see an acupuncturist.

That doctor visit ended up being one of the most enlightening experiences I've had. He first conducted a series of tests to see the sensitive areas of her energy bodies. The tests were administered with little vials of liquids. If her body was sensitive to what was in the vial, her muscles would become weak and she couldn't resist his pull. We discovered that she didn't have any more allergies; however, there were things that she was sensitive to, such as cold air, corn, and chicken.

Before he started the acupuncture treatment, he explained where he would put the needles and described the various pressure points. I learned that the pressure points that balanced the stomach were found in her arms, stomach area, and hands. He also placed needles in her head, ears, and feet. It's interesting to understand how our body is connected through energies and that certain pressure points can balance or unclog those energies. Along with the treatment, he also provided mental strategies for her healing. He told her that when she felt nauseous, she should start thinking and repeating the word "down."

An hour and a half later, we left the office. Over the next couple of days, I watched and waited anxiously for any signs of sickness. None came, and three years later, she's still healthy. It was the end of the seven-year nightmare.

That day, I came to understand, like never before, the power of the connectivity of our mind, body, and spirit, and how the body can be restored when disturbances in the appropriate energy field are removed. Also, I could see that my daughter felt empowered in thinking that she had some type of control over her health for the first time. She made a decision that she was through being sick. She learned how to balance her mind, body, and spirit. I share this story not only to reinforce the teachings about the body and its energy and the power of the mind, but also to encourage you to seek out alternative options if you have a sickness.

Thinking Your Way to Better Health

As stated previously, your body, mind, and spirit are all connected and therefore affect each other. Your mind can negatively and positively impact your health, such as is the story of Donna.

Donna invited me to do an interview on her cable television show. We scheduled a day and time for me to talk about emotional wellness on the topic of "successful aging." When I arrived, she began to brief me about the show and the expectations. When the taping began, I noticed that she was more reserved than most hosts, although quite pleasant. She mentioned the dying process on a couple of occasions and I made a mental note that she had experienced something in that area.

After the show, I asked her how she came to host the show. She said she started and hosted the show voluntarily because she saw a need. She shared with me that she changed her thoughts and how she viewed life after being diagnosed with degenerative lung disease, an illness with no known cause, treatment, or cure. Her doctors has told her that she could die any day.

She explained what it was like knowing that your life may be ending at any time. She was confused and shocked, but decided to make some very important choices regarding her health. She began by modifying her diet; adding an exercise plan; and creating strategies to manage her breathing. However, the biggest adjustment took place in her mind and thoughts. Although she was determined to fight for her life, the reality of the diagnosis prompted her to start planning her funeral. As she talked, I visualized this vibrant young woman talking to a funeral director about her services and her burial plot. It took a minute for me to regroup from that visual and from the thoughts of what that must have been like. She decided to change her thoughts and the people in her life, and focus on things that mattered. Instead of focusing on death and dying, she decided that she would focus on living. She embraced life; ran for mayor of her city; created a magazine; and continues to change lives with her TV show. What a lesson! I thought I was going to share my expertise on emotional wellness with her and the audience, and while I accomplished my task, I also walked away a different person having witnessed how her thoughts have changed her health and her way of living.

Positive Thoughts to Ponder

Thoughts

- You weren't born with any limits on your powers or any set limits to your capacity.
- You can't do everything, but you can do something.
- Your success is but a determined action away.
- Your life will always be what you make of it. Your thoughts and actions will lead you to success or failure. So the keys to your success and fortune are in your hands.

- You can have anything on earth that you want, once you mentally accept the fact that you can have it.
- Your own positive energy will compel things to turn out the way you desire when you're surrounded by positive people.
- You can't be a winner and be afraid to lose.
- You don't need more strength or more ability or greater opportunity.
- What you need is to use what you have.
- Learn to seize good fortune, for it is always around you.
- People with goals succeed because they know where they are going.

Quotes

- "You are today where your thoughts have brought you; you will be tomorrow where your thoughts take you."—James Allen, author and philosopher
- "People become really quite remarkable when they start thinking they can do things."—Norman Vincent Peale, author
- "The winners in life think constantly in terms of I can, I will, and I am. Losers, on the other hand, concentrate their waking thoughts on what they should have or would have done, or what they can't do."—Denis Waitley, author
- "Whatever the mind can conceive and believe, it can achieve riches."—Napoleon Hill, author

REST STOP

It's time to take a look at your thoughts. This exercise will help you to identify the thoughts that constantly invade your mind.

Make a list of your negative thoughts. For each of the negative thoughts, list beside it a positive one. This exercise will not only make you aware of your negative thoughts but help you to consciously think of positive thoughts to replace the negative. Example:

Negative	**Positive**
1. I am unreliable.	1. I am learning to be dependable.
2. I am ugly.	2. I am beautiful.
3. I can't believe I did that.	3. I will learn from that.
4. I can't do anything right.	4. Every day in every way, I'm getting better and better.

Roadmap

Brighten your thinking.

1. **Never underestimate the power of your thoughts.** As has been discussed and proven for centuries, your thoughts can:
   - help or hurt you;
   - create positive or negative energy;
   - make you happy or sad;
   - make you sick or well;
   - create friends or enemies;
   - make you laugh or cry;
   - hold you back or move you forward; and
   - help you succeed or fail.
2. **Stay away from negative people**. Negative people bring negative thoughts, attitudes, and energy. They pollute your mind and can hold you down. Chapter 9 is dedicated to dealing with toxic people.
3. **Go on a positive thought diet**. Make a commitment not to watch negative programs, or to watch, listen, or read negative news. Refuse to talk negatively about people or listen to other

people talk negatively. You will find that things will look and feel peaceful and you will feel lighter on your feet. Negativity brings about strife and adds heaviness to your life.

4. **Read uplifting books and articles.** There are many books that have been written that focus on positive thoughts. My favorites include:
   - *Power of Positive Thinking* by Norman Vincent Peale
   - *Think and Grow Rich* by Napoleon Hill
   - *The Law of Attraction* by Jerry Hicks

5. **Start a gratitude journal**. Write down three things a day that you are grateful for. This will help your thoughts focus on what you have, not on what you don't have.

6. **Start your day with positive affirmations/meditation**. Find five of your favorite quotes, print them out, and tape them to your bathroom wall, in your car, and on the refrigerator. When you inundate your mind with positive and uplifting thoughts, it will flood your body and soul with energy. (See a list of quotes in the "Positive Thoughts to Ponder" sidebar earlier in this chapter.)

SIX

Traffic Jams: Your Words Can Cause Fender-Benders, Gridlock, or Worse

Controlling Your Tongue

L ET'S FACE IT, nobody likes traffic jams. And, when you encounter one, it doesn't matter what has caused the jam, because the effect is a delay in reaching your destination, with potential consequences like missed meetings, missed flights, or annoyed friends. Likewise, certain things you say can inhibit you, or others, from reaching set goals. It's essential to understand that words can have both positive *and* negative impacts.

When Cole first tried out for the junior league football team, he could hardly catch the ball and didn't make the team. His dad tried to console him by saying that not everyone is athletic, but Cole's feelings were hurt because he really liked football and wanted to learn the sport. His dad told him not to waste his time. So Cole didn't try out again, but he did keep playing at the park with friends. By his sophomore year, he knew that he had a shot at the team, but his dad still told him to give up the idea. During his senior year, Cole finally asked the coach to watch a video of him playing football. The coach was amazed and told

Cole that he was a natural and that he could have been a star player. Unfortunately, his dad's words had stopped him from taking action.

This chapter examines the strength of words. The first section will look at the damage or blockages that words can cause. The next section will focus on how to take control of your words and use them to uplift and empower yourself and others. With this revelation, my hope is that you will begin to use your words to project positive thoughts and energy into everyone and every situation that arises along your journey.

Words That Tear Down

We have all heard the saying, "Sticks and stones may break my bones, but words will never hurt me." Those words rang out over the play-ground when I was growing up. I even recited the phrase when I was on the receiving end of taunts from my classmates. However, I have since learned that the statement cannot be further from the truth. Words can cause lasting damage to one's self-esteem. I work with clients who, after thirty years, are still trying to "get over" words said to them in child-hood. The wounds from hurtful words can be more painful than phys-ical trauma, and the scars can be far deeper.

"You are fat and ugly, and nobody will ever want you!" Susan heard these words repeatedly from her father as she was growing up. He convinced her that she was almost worthless, and her self-esteem was severely impacted. At age sixty-one, she finally sought help for some issues she was dealing with and called me. When I began to examine some of her past decisions with men, she shared with me the words that had been playing in her head since childhood; she still believed her father's hurtful words. She had been married a few times and was in and out of relationships. Her first husband, like her father, was emotionally abusive to her. You can imagine the work that it takes for someone like Susan to heal. Erasing the ugliness of the words that had haunted her entire life required Susan to confront the pain and reprogram her mind to create positive thoughts.

For some people, it takes only *one* negative word to disturb their spirit, which sometimes erases numerous positive words. Because we are programmed to care about what others think and have a desire to be accepted and liked, a negative comment can be unsettling. Here's a prime example: when I first started my speaking career, I handed out evaluation sheets at the end of my presentations. I would get back thirty evaluations that talked about how great and fabulous I was as a speaker, but it was the handful of negative comments that always stuck with me: "She talked too fast," "Didn't get much from the session," "She was excessively energetic," etc. My mind would fixate on those comments. Never mind that thirty others had just sworn that I hung the moon. My spirit was uneasy because I placed more value on those negative comments, than I did on the positive.

Words Can Kill and Destroy

Words can also kill. Bullying itself, treating others abusively, is nothing new; the practice has been around for thousands of years—perhaps even since the beginning of civilization. But bullying has taken on a different form in today's culture and the practice is reaching epidemic levels. About 160,000 children miss school every day because they are afraid of being bullied. Even more staggering is the statistic that 8 percent of children under the age of fourteen commit suicide because of bullying—a phenomenon known as "bullycide" that unfortunately has come to prominence in recent years. Hurtful and demeaning words are not only said and heard at school but now are spread over the Internet and through text messages.

Words can also destroy reputations. I am certain that, if you are like me, you've thought about sending a letter to your foe—a cease and desist of all negative conversation about you—at one point in your life. To hear that someone is spreading lies about you, even within a small circle of people, can enrage you. I once had a conversation with a woman who had met one of my former business associates. The woman causally began to tell me what my former associate had said about me. Not one word that he had said was true, and I felt my temperature begin to rise. How could he have said such things? I have never been able to understand how people can perpetuate lies, and I immediately wanted to call him and give him a piece of my mind. But, after I thought it through and slept on it, I decided that it wasn't worth my time or energy.

This kind of behavior is only a taste of what some celebrities have to go through on a daily basis. Imagine walking into a bookstore and seeing your picture plastered on the front cover of gossip magazines along with a bogus headline. Because it is in print, the human mind wants to believe that it's true. When people perceive something to be true, they will spread toxic words to others, and, true or not, it's damaging to reputations.

Words can tear us down in many ways, but we need to focus on restoring and rebuilding the mind and spirit from those damaging words.

REST STOP

In your Amazing Life notebook, make a list of words that are your triggers. These are the words that, if said to or about you, would prompt an emotional response—words like "control freak," "emotional," "naïve," "angry," "bitter," "workaholic," etc. For example, when people used to say to me, "You always have to be right," it bothered me because I didn't think that about myself.

Once you've created your list, look over the words to see if there's any truth to them. If there's a bit of truth, then there's room for improvement. For instance, when I thought about it, who doesn't want to be right? However, the connotation to that comment wasn't positive. It meant that I always had to prove my point at all costs. So I did need to modify my behavior to a point. If there's some truth to the words, you'll become defensive when you hear them. This is your clue that you need to take a deeper look at your behavior. If there's no truth to the words, just say to yourself, "I'm not _____; you are dismissed." That means you are assigning zero value and energy to that word.

ROAD TO RECOVERY FROM DAMAGING WORDS

As we have established, words can hurt, but how do you heal from hurtful words? Here are strategies and techniques that you can implement to help you recover from the powerful impact of negative words.

1. **Know, understand, and accept that people are going to talk about you.** Like it or not, this is a part of life. Understand that there's not a lot that you can do about the negative things that people say. Every human being on the face of the planet, at one time or another, will be talked about by others. The true gift is learning how to respond to these words. You can't control other people, but you can control your response. This simple fact of life is something to teach your children that could help them deal with bullying or teasing. For detailed information on how to teach your children to deal with bullying, go to my Web site, www.creatingamazinglives.com, to download a free booklet.

2. **Learn to assign appropriate value and energy to words.** I know you've heard the saying, "If the shoe fits, wear it." It's really an appropriate quote for this technique. If someone's saying things about you that aren't true, don't give it value or energy. I know it's easier said than done, but you can practice the technique of dismissing words using the simple method of finding and repeating three positive adjectives that will replace the negative one. Focus your mind on the positive words.

3. **Never let other people's words define you.** It's important for you to know who you are. When you know who you are and feel good about yourself, you can ward off negative words. Continue to build your confidence and the words will bounce off of you like a rubber ball.

4. **Build a thick skin.** Since you already know that you are going to be talked about, lighten up on the emotions. Building a thick skin is kind of like building muscle through weight lifting. Learn to let negative feedback roll off your back.

5. **Practice the art of forgiveness**. Words that cut you deeply when you were a child, teenager, young adult, or adult will only be released through the art of forgiveness. This practice is so significant to your emotional health and wellness and your spiritual balance that I will cover it in depth in Chapter 13.

6. **Give others the benefit of the doubt**. Sometimes, a person's words may hurt you, but that might not have been their intention. The commenter was likely trying to offer some constructive feedback—cut them some slack.

7. **Use wit and humor**. When possible, use humor to fight negative words. I am fortunate to have a good sense of humor. One of the techniques I developed to defend myself against my childhood bullies was a quick wit. I was also quite a talker; it's a skill that comes in handy when deflecting negativity, much like comedians do when they are confronted with a heckler. I am not saying that you have to be a comedian, just don't take things too seriously.

Using Words to Empower Yourself and Others

You speak your reality: just as your thoughts become your actions, so do your words. While your thoughts and words are connected, your words become more dominant. You can have a thought and dismiss it, but once a word is spoken, try as you might, it can't be retracted. You can try to "strike it from the record" or apologize or both, but once it comes out, it's out and it can't be erased from the memory. Thoughts are private, yet words become public declarations. In Chapter 5, we discussed your thoughts as the foundation for who you are and where you are in life. Changing your thoughts may be the start to achieving success, but your words are the legs that carry you toward success or failure.

Now, instead of focusing on just positive thinking, we are going to talk about the importance of positive word affirmations. Let me explain how affirmations work. You have to convince your subconscious that what you are saying is true. If you have constantly told yourself that you are not that smart, your subconscious believes you. You have to continue to repeat "I am smart" in order for your conscious mind to believe it. It may feel uncomfortable at first since you *believe* that you aren't smart, but the positive word affirmation will begin to affirm a belief in your subconscious and the negative thoughts will be replaced with the positive ones. When you experience a sense of joy and well-being, your mind instinctively responds to something it believes to be true. When you feel this emotion, you know your affirmations are working!

In order for you to believe your words, you need to repeat them out loud. As humans, we learn through repetition of information and words. Think how many times you sang The ABC Song as a child. Even though you know the alphabet so well, if I were to ask you to recite the alphabet backward, it would be hard for you to do. You would have to stop and really think about it. You didn't learn it backward through repetition, so it's not stored in your subconscious that way.

Repetition is required to empower yourself with words. In the last few years, I have heard discussions and read articles that discuss the role that self-talk plays in life, as well as the effectiveness of repeating and affirming positive words. This is effective because words affect inner and outer energy bodies. As I pointed out in Chapter 5, one of the phrases that I repeat to myself several times a day is, "Every day, in every way, I am getting better and better." In order for that mantra to change my actions, I have to really believe in what I am saying. Another one of my affirmations comes from a biblical text: "I can do all things through Christ who strengthens me." These two declarations affirm that I can achieve anything.

REST STOP

What are your word affirmations? Create a list of affirmations that you can repeat to yourself on a daily basis. You can use the below suggestions or make up your own.

- I am a winner.
- Things will get better today.
- I deserve the best.
- I am excellent.
- I can lose the weight.
- I can be healthy.
- I am going to be rich.
- I am beautiful.
- I am smart.
- What I say makes an impact.
- I love and embrace life.

- -

Take Control of *Your* Words

Since you can't control what other people do or say, I want to focus on how you can control the words that you say. I remember a plaque at my great grandmother's house that read "Be careful of the words you say / keep them kind and sweet / you never know from day to day / which ones you'll have to eat." There was also a knife and a fork on the plaque for the full effect. That saying has stayed with me throughout my life. Most of us learned word control in elementary school, but it seems so many adults have forgotten the simple rules, which I outline below.

1. **Think before you speak.** You don't have to say everything that you think.
2. **If you don't have something good to say, don't say anything at all.** That should about eliminate one-third of people's daily conversations.
3. **Don't say anything about someone that you can't repeat to his or her face.**

4. Count to five before you respond.
5. Don't talk when others are talking.
6. Say to others what you would want them to say to you.

Before you decide that you need to say what's on your mind or spread words that were just repeated to you, ask yourself these two questions:

1. Is what I am going to say a benefit or of value to the listener?
2. Will it make the listener feel better or worse?

I can almost guarantee that at least half of the things that you want to repeat or tell someone won't pass the test.

Speak Words That Edify

Since we have talked a great deal about how words can tear you down, I want to focus on how words can build you up. I have heard many stories of people who, because their parent(s), teacher, friend, or mentor believed in them, they were able to succeed in life. Sometimes people attribute their success to others believing in them when they didn't believe in themselves. Sometimes all it takes is one person saying something positive that sticks with you. Sometimes the words spoken may not seem positive at the time, but look at the person who is speaking and the spirit in which the words are meant.

Such is the case with the following story about my mother. I remember when my mother made a declaration about me that hurt at the time, yet her intent was meant to build me up. In one of our usual weekly family meetings, she decided to tell her children the talents and gifts that she thought we possessed. Being the youngest of three girls, I had to wait for my turn. She started with my older sister, Sarita, and told her, "You can sing so beautifully; your voice sounds like a bird. It is so melodious. You also have the talent of being able to sew and make clothes with the perfection of a tailor. And you are smart. You do so well in school. You are just so gifted!"

Now keep in mind I could also sing and I was making all of my clothes as well. So I was anxiously waiting to hear some of the same compliments. Next was my middle sister, Tina, who really was *super* smart. My mother told her, "You are so smart. I am so proud of your accomplishments. You are in the National Honor Society, the debate team, speech, and forensics. You are class president. You are a good leader, and a great student. You are extremely gifted!"

I could hardly wait to hear what my mother thought my special gifts were. When it was finally my turn, she looked me and said, "Lawana, you have the *gift of gab*." That's it? Nothing else? It was painful. All my life, all I heard year after year in school were the infamous words, "She talks too much!" So how could I possibly think that having the "gift of gab" was truly a gift? My mother never meant to hurt my feelings, but her words stung me. Fast forward a few years and this gab gift is now the way that I make a living. Instead of holding that against my mother and feeling defeated because she didn't point out how smart I was or how beautifully I could sing or sew clothes, I was able to take my gift and run.

I'm Okay, You're Okay

A friend recently shared with me that she didn't feel great about herself when she was growing up and going through adolescence. All of her friends were working and were able to buy clothes, but she wasn't. When she compared herself to others, she didn't feel as cute; she was bigger in size and just didn't feel like she measured up. Then she saw a commercial on TV that said, "I'm okay, you're okay." She took those words and wrapped them around her mind, repeated them, and believed them. This was her turning point. Today she's a very successful school administrator in a district where she reminds kids every day that they are okay the way they are.

Ways to Encourage Others

Here are practices that will help you encourage others in your life:

Parents—Make it a habit to say something positive to your child every day. Tell them what they mean to you, how wonderful they are, etc. Even if they don't act wonderful all the time, they need to understand that you love them not because of how they act, but because of who they are. There is an incredible difference between the two.

Friends—Share with your friends how much value they bring to your life. Be open about and freely share with them their positive characteristics. Support them and their dreams. One of my mentors, Myron Golden, practices a great habit that I will pass on to you in the hope that that you will implement it into your conversations with the people that you care about.

When I call him on the phone, the conversation goes like this:

Me: Hello, how are you?
Myron: Excellent as always; better now that I am talking to you.

If he is already excellent and you make him feel even better, that is some power. That greeting not only makes you smile but it makes you feel important, too.

Colleagues—Spread sunshine at work. I know that may be difficult, because frankly I know you don't like everyone that you work with. However, it's not about others; it's about you. What are you projecting? Say "good morning" to everyone. Approach each day in the office with a positive attitude in spite of what may have transpired the day before. Remember that today is a new day. Respect those that you work with, even though you may think some don't deserve it. If you don't have something good to say, don't say anything at all. Just smile and nod over your cup of coffee.

Strangers—Make it your business to smile at everyone. I know some of you are not natural-born "smilers," but it takes more muscles to frown than smile. A free gesture takes one second but can make a lasting impression. I have actually been told that I smile too much and that sometimes that can be an invitation or send the wrong message to a person. I am not as concerned with that as I am in wanting everyone to know that for that moment, I am happy. I want everyone that I meet to feel better having met me. Challenge yourself to the same thing. It will change your life.

Roadmap

1. **Make a commitment to use your words to bring value to yourself and others**. You can see how powerful words are. Decide that you will use your words to build up people and not tear them down.

2. **Watch your words**. Tell a friend or spouse to help you watch what you say. If you speak negative words, have them use the code word "switch." That will help you flip the switch to something positive.

3. **Heal yourself**. Work to get over damaging words. If you were hurt by someone's words, work hard to flush it out of your thoughts and subconscious. Work on healing yourself with the tips and strategies that are offered in this chapter.

4. **Positive thoughts will align with positive words**. In the previous chapter we discussed how important positive thoughts are, and the same holds true for positive words. They work hand in hand. If you keep your mind clean and happy, your words automatically will flow the same way.

5. **Do your part to influence others**. Don't allow people in your presence to speak negative words about themselves or others. Tell them that words have energy and you want to keep your space filled with positive energy. Doing this helps you to take control of your environment.

SEVEN

Road Rage

Managing Your Emotions

"GET OUT OF THE WAY, you stupid idiot! Learn how to drive or get a bicycle!"

Perhaps you've heard people angrily shouting words like these at other drivers on the road. It's likely you have experienced a bit of road rage at one point or another from someone who drove up behind you too close, excessively honked the horn at you, shouted expletives at you, or gave vulgar hand gestures. On the other hand, maybe you are the one that shouts at other drivers, always blows your horn, rides too close to the back bumper, or flashes your lights.

One road rage experience that frightened me the most was when a driver thought that I had cut him off, so he quickly got in front of me and slammed on his brakes. I had to slam on mine to avoid hitting him and then he took off. I was so livid at that moment, but the anger I felt quickly dissolved into relief when I realized that I had avoided an accident.

Road rage is quite an epidemic these days and it's a reflection of how stressed we feel as a society. But, as with many other forms of stress, we can control our stress levels on the road and in our lives. It's imperative that we do so, because stress can take enormous physical and mental tolls on our bodies. According to the American Psychological Association, about 94 percent of adults believe that stress can contribute to the development of major illnesses, such as heart disease, depression, and obesity. Stress also relates to your emotions. A recent study by the

World Health Organization (WHO) found that 66 percent of American employees report that they have difficulty focusing on tasks at work because of stress. WHO tagged stress as the United States' "health epidemic of the twenty-first century"; the effects of stress are estimated to cost American companies close to $300 billion a year.

Since you're in control of your emotions and your response to stress, you have a level of control over your physical health. In this chapter, we will look at emotions and stress and how they impact your overall well-being. I will offer tips and strategies that will help you look at and deal with your emotions and stress in a different way. The goal of this chapter is to help you achieve emotional wellness.

What Are Emotions?

Emotions are mental states that arise spontaneously rather than through conscious effort and are often accompanied by physiological changes, like a racing heart when you're nervous or laughter when you're happy. Emotions are a cornerstone of behaviors and motivations; our ability to experience them is what makes us human. Emotions are extremely critical to our overall well-being. I believe that an introduction of emotional intelligence (*below*) is beneficial.

Emotional Intelligence

Peter Salovey and John D. Mayer, the leading researchers of *emotional intelligence* (EI) have defined it as the ability to identify, assess, and control your emotions, as well as the emotions of others. It's critical to managing your behavior, moving smoothly through social situations, and making critical choices in life. There are four components to emotional intelligence—self-awareness, self-management, social awareness, and relationship management. These components are grouped into two categories: personal competence, which is the focus on you individually, your self-awareness, and self-management skills; and social competence, which is your social awareness and relationship management skills.

PERSONAL COMPETENCY
- **Self-awareness** is how accurately you can identify your emotions in the moment and understand your tendencies across time and situation.
- **Self-management** is how you use awareness of your emotions to create the behavior that you want.

SOCIAL COMPETENCY
- **Social awareness** is how well you read the emotions of other people.
- **Relationship management** is how you use the first three emotional intelligence skills to manage your interactions with other people.

Where Do Emotions Come From?

Let's look at where your emotions originate. They are a part of the limbic system of your brain. The limbic system manages your emotions, hormones, urges, passion, and temperature control. The majority of decisions we make are driven by emotions. Your neo-cortex or "rational brain" is where logic and reasoning are processed, but the limbic system (the "emotional brain") reacts to events first, before you have the opportunity to engage the rational brain. Here's a prime example of how your emotional brain reacts before your rational brain kicks in:

Sixteen-year-old Lydia was thrilled to finally be able to drive like all of her friends. She was happy to go to the nearest pizza place and pick up a pizza for dinner. In her haste to park, she slightly nipped the car next to her. Her instant reaction brought a flood of tears. She was afraid and couldn't think of what to do. Her friend, who was riding with her, encouraged her to stop crying, calm down, and call her mother. Her friend was able to get Lydia to calm down so she could think rationally. She was able to engage her brain rationally so she could be coherent when the police officer arrived.

In other cases, when a person is unable to calm down and manage their emotions, they are unable to make the switch to their logical brain. Emotional intelligence requires effective communication between the rational and emotional centers of the brain. It is important to understand that emotional intelligence has a massive impact upon your personal and professional successes.

Now, let's look at *emotional wellness* (EW) and how it compares to EI.

Emotional Wellness

Emotional wellness digs a bit deeper than emotional intelligence. It's the intentional effort made to becoming healthy in terms of mind, spirit, and emotions. It's the complete recognition of your full range of feelings, both positive and negative, and your ability to handle them. While EI focuses on your personal emotions, it also includes assessing other people's emotions. EW is all about managing your own self—your body and spirit. Emotions are a part of who you are, how you think, your behavior, and the motivation behind your actions. And having emotional wellness is not only necessary for keeping you from rear-ending the car in front of you out of road rage, but it's also a prerequisite for having an amazing life. Emotional wellness—and thus an amazing life—happens when you have good health in mind, body, and spirit.

MIND, BODY, AND SPIRIT—THREE IN ONE
Although the human body is infinitely complex and contains many moving parts, the totality of who we are consists of mind, body, and spirit, which are all interconnected. The mind is composed of your thoughts and emotions. The way you think and feel dictates how you live your life. Your body is your physical being that responds and reacts to your mind, your thoughts, and emotions. And your spirit

is the moral fiber of who you are. Your mind, body, and spirit work together to create stability in your life, which happens when they are in balance; if they are not, you have disequilibrium or imbalance. If your mind is unhealthy and filled with unresolved pain or anger, so is your body and spirit. If your spirit is unhealthy, it will affect your mind and your body. If your body is unhealthy, it can affect your mind and spirit. As we work toward strategies that will help you achieve EW, we will first explore how emotions affect men and women differently.

The Emotional Affect: Men vs. Women

In examining emotions, it's necessary to understand the differences between men and women—their feelings, reactions, and control techniques. Not only will knowing the differences educate you in the human brain, but it will help you to better relate to the opposite sex. When you hear that someone was emotional, you'd probably assume it was a woman. In addition to the cultural programming differences of boys and girls and their taught response to feelings, the male and female brains are wired differently, but that doesn't mean only women experience emotions. Men have emotions, too!

Just think about how it was for you growing up, or, if you are a parent, the difference in raising boys and girls. From the time they are toddlers little boys are conditioned not to cry and to always be a "big boy" when they fall and hurt themselves. Meanwhile, little girls are encouraged to have feelings and express themselves. Young girls are conditioned that it's all right to cry and feel and they are often encouraged to do so. Many of the differences in the way men and women experience emotions stem from variations in the physical makeup of the brains in each gender. To understand this, we'll explore the basic composition of the brain and how it varies in men and women.

THE LIMBIC SYSTEM

As you may recall, the limbic system controls your emotions and hormones. Women typically have a larger limbic system than men do, which allows them to be more in touch with their feelings and better able to express them, making it possible for them to bond with others with greater ease. Because of this ability to connect, more women serve as caregivers for children. The down side to this larger limbic system is that it also leaves women more vulnerable to depression, especially during times of hormonal shifts. Because the male limbic system is smaller, they aren't as aware or in touch with their feelings.

THE HIPPOCAMPUS

The hippocampus is the memory center. When an emotional event passes, women tend to hold on to the memory, whereas men tend to let it go. The hippocampus is larger in women and has more neural pathways connecting it to emotive centers, which is the reason why women remember emotional events more than men do. A man will remember less of his emotional experiences than a woman will. For example, he will remember the details of a car he wanted to purchase, but probably won't hold on to the emotional meaning of his first job.

THE AMYGDALA

The amygdala is the section of the brain that handles aggression as well as the emotional connection to events. Brain research of the amygdala has found that when men and women were exposed to pictures of sad or frightened people and asked to imagine what they were thinking, their amygdala lights up. Researchers note that the men's amygdala shut down after a few minutes and then higher cortical functions light up. This indicates that men simply do not hold on to emotional responses very long before searching for a *rational* response to process the emotion. The female brain lingers longer on the negative feelings—hence, the differences in how men and women handle grief. Men will move more quickly to the practical side of things as opposed to lingering on the actual death.

It's significant to note these gender differences in the brain, because it helps to explain the discrepancy in how men and women process, respond, and react to things, situations, and people. In the end, everyone is responsible for managing his or her emotions. To help you make a deliberate effort every day to manage your emotions, it's vital to prepare yourself in the best way every day to manage what life events you may have to face. You need start each day knowing your EW number.

Know Your EW Number

There are several wellness campaigns that emphasize the importance of knowing your EW numbers: measuring cholesterol, blood pressure, blood sugar, and BMI. By knowing your numbers, you can take action to make positive changes that will help prevent the onset of or treat chronic health conditions. The same goes for your emotional health. For your next Rest Stop exercise, I have created a simple set of questions that will allow you to monitor your emotional wellness every day.

Start each day with this simple test. There are two questions from each category that will basically indicate your present state of being.

Mind

1. I feel good about myself today.	Yes	No
2. I am passionate about living today.	Yes	No

Body

1. I got adequate sleep last night	Yes	No
2. I ate breakfast this morning	Yes	No

Spirit

1. I have integrated prayer, meditation, yoga, or quiet time
   into my day.   Yes   No
2. I have made someone else's life better today.   Yes   No

For each yes, give yourself 2 points and for each no give yourself a 0. I'm sure you are thinking, *A zero?* That's right. You don't get any points for no's because any one of the no's can and will affect your day and your overall emotional well-being. The ideal score to reach each day is 12. You should strive to get a "yes" in all categories every day. A yes to each question will put you at your maximum potential energy level that is humanly possible to achieve. Now I realize that from day to day, and sometimes hour by hour, your emotions can change, and while you started out enjoying the day, by three o'clock in the afternoon, it's turning into one of the worst days. However, know that you **can** pull your emotions back to a positive place by following the techniques in the next section

ROAD TO MANAGING YOUR EMOTIONS

1. **Be aware of and respect your emotions**. You know there are several emotions/feelings that you can experience in one day. Accept that you will have positive and negative feelings each day. Being aware of and accepting your feelings will help you increase your sensitivity to your own feelings.
2. **Acknowledge your feelings and the causes**. As in the prior exercise, recognize the emotion that you are feeling. Identify the emotion and then assign a reason for it. Think about what caused you to feel that way. Was something said or done that caused you to feel this way?
3. **Ask yourself, "Is that feeling valid?"** You can create unfounded emotions when you heard or thought you heard someone say

something about you. This happens when people spread lies about each other. Be careful of your interpretations of what you *think* others meant by what they said. It's easy to take things out of context and get in a negative space because of what you *thought* they meant by what they said.

4. **You don't have to act the way you feel.** Even though you may be upset or angry with something or someone, it doesn't mean that you have to act on your feelings. It's possible to feel anger and express anger without being disrespectful, violent, or abusive.

5. **Refocus your negative feelings on positive thoughts.** When something negative happens, look for the unseen benefit. For example, if you're upset because you got passed over for the promotion and you feel with all your heart that it should have been you, focus your energy instead on the fact that you still have a job and start planning for the future. Figure out how you can best position yourself for the next promotion or perhaps another job.

6. **Don't react when you're upset.** Whatever you have to say can and should wait until you calm down and are in control of your emotions. Otherwise, you run the risk of saying something that you'll regret and can't take back.

7. **Sleep on it.** When you're feeling a set of emotions because of an action that made you upset—an email, a situation, a decision, a conversation—don't respond until you've had a good night's rest. You'll be surprised what sleep will do for your brain and your emotions.

8. **Create a safe place to release your emotions.** Releasing your emotions at work, or another public place, is not the answer. Instead, do something or go somewhere where you can safely release your feelings: talk to a trusted friend; write in a journal; start a hobby; play a sport or exercise; find a place where you can scream.

Stress, the Colossal Enemy to Your Health

"Stress" is a word that everyone, including children, are familiar with. I found this to be the case with my client Michelle, who at an early age, would always hear her mother say, "You are stressing me out." Since she was a child, she didn't quite understand what that meant, but it didn't sound good. At nine years old, Michelle started repeating that she was stressed because she didn't understand some of her homework. Ever since then, Michelle has felt that stress has been a big factor in her life and she came to me to try to figure out how to reduce stress in her life.

She's not alone in this struggle. As mentioned in the introduction to this chapter, stress is a major epidemic in our culture and a huge factor in terms of your emotional wellness. According to the American Psychological Association (APA), the top reasons for stress include:

1. Job pressure
2. Money
3. Health
4. Relationships
5. Poor nutrition
6. Media overload
7. Sleep deprivation

Because stress is a major factor in determining your health, there's a great deal of research that has been done to examine its impact on our lives. The data collected from general population studies done by the APA and the American Institute of Stress indicates that:

- 77 percent of the general population experience physical symptoms caused by stress.
- 73 percent experience psychological symptoms caused by stress.
- 76 percent cited money and work as the leading cause of their stress.

This colossal enemy is having an impact on the lives of most humans in a major way. Not a day goes by that many of us don't experience the effects of stress. Researchers at the APA took a look at how stress affects people in their daily lives. The results are as follows:

- 48 percent say stress has a negative impact on their personal and professional life.
- 54 percent say stress has caused them to fight with people close to them.
- 48 percent reported overeating or eating unhealthy foods to manage stress, while one in four skipped a meal in the last month because of stress. Poor eating habits have resulted in higher rates of obesity.
- One out of every five Americans reported drinking alcohol to manage their stress and 16 percent reported smoking.
- Stress causes more than 850 thousand deaths a year.

As you can see, stress takes a toll on your emotional and physical health. Many people experience physical symptoms without realizing that stress is the cause. Some of the physical signs of stress include fatigue, headaches, an upset stomach, muscle tension, a change in appetite, teeth grinding, a change in sex drive, or feeling dizzy. On the other hand, the psychological symptoms of stress affect your emotions and make you feel irritable or angry, nervous, lethargic, and sad.

Is Your Job "Stressing You Out"?

How would you honestly answer that question? Some of the causes of workplace stress include low salaries; lack of advancement or growth opportunities; heavy workload; long hours; and uncertain or undefined job expectations. The stress that's experienced on the job is often caused by situations or circumstances that you may not have control over. It causes an additional layer of stress when you feel that someone else is controlling your life.

A study done by the APA in 2013 about the direct effects of on-the-job stress revealed the following findings:

- 30 percent of employees report feeling stressed out during their workday.
- 31 percent of employed adults have difficulty managing work and family responsibilities.
- 75 to 90 percent of all physician office visits are for stress-related ailments and complaints.
- $300 billion is the annual cost to employers for their employees' stress-related health care and missed work.

Everyday stress combined with work-place stress creates a huge problem. Stress has been linked to the six leading causes of death—heart disease, cancer, lung ailments, accidents, cirrhosis of the liver, and suicide. Knowing this information helps you to understand that if you don't manage your stress, it can kill you.

Reacting to Stress in a Good Way

It's vitally important that you listen to your body and take steps to prevent unnecessary stress. Many times, your body will send signals such as aches, pains, headaches, and fatigue as signs that you need to regroup. Such was the case with Trina. She was "super stressed" because of her job. She was a recent hire and felt the need to prove her worth. To add to her anxiety, she had a boss that really didn't do his job well. He would shift his responsibilities to her while trying to make himself look good to his manager. Trina was working hard to handle her workload with an insufficient amount of training. She was working long hours and feeling overwhelmed with trying to manage it all.

I first worked with her to integrate the stress relief techniques listed in the next section. We also had to create a communication plan for how to approach her boss with her concerns. In the end, through confidence-building activities and other strategies, Trina learned how to control what she could, release the rest, and find a sense of peace and balance with her job.

REST STOP

In your notebook, make a list of all the things that contribute to your stress each day. How many things made it on your list? Did your list include work, finances, health care, traffic, sleep, gas prices, work/life balance, marriage, or children? Now look at your list and cross off the things that made your list that you cannot control. Follow the first two steps in the following roadmap to help you manage your list.

ROAD TO MANAGING YOUR STRESS

1. **Don't stress over things you can't control.** I am certain you have heard that before, but are you following the rule? Look back at your list and check off the things you can't control. Your list should get increasingly smaller. Stop stressing over the state of the economy. You can't fix it, so don't waste your energy talking about it. If implemented in your life, this tip should alleviate the majority of your stress.

2. **Focus your energy on what you *can* control.** Since you only have a certain amount of energy each day, use it on the controllable things in your life, such as your health, finances, and relationships. Make a plan to make those areas of your life better, as discussed in Chapter 2.

3. **Create more balance in your life by deleting at least one activity from your schedule.** Look at the schedule for your life. The work/life balance could mean that you are just doing too much. Do you really need to be involved in every project or volunteer opportunity? Do your kids have to be in three extracurricular activities? What causes you to feel overwhelmed or constantly feel like you're spinning out of control? Let go of at least one of the activities that you're involved in. There was a time when I looked at my life, and

thought, *I can't possibly be productive, because I'm doing too much.* Although it was prestigious and an honor to be on the board of this or that organization, I realized that when I took it off my plate, it freed up an extra twenty-five to thirty hours a month.

4. **Make family a priority over your job.** When you're neglecting what you say is the most important part of your life, your family, you're going to feel stressed and off-balanced. Make whatever changes you need to make sure that your family doesn't feel neglected.

5. **Learn to say NO.** So many people continue to share with me that saying "no" is one of their biggest struggles. When you say yes and really want to say no, stress attacks all the fibers of your being. You are going against your mind and emotions, and your body will react. When you have a plan for your life, it's easy to say no, because what you are being asked to do doesn't fit into your plan. Of course, if you're following along with this book, you will have planned and set boundaries for things and people in your life. However, to help you along, go to a mirror right now and practice saying the word "no" with a smile. It is not a bad word. It's actually a good one.

6. **Incorporate exercise in your routine.** Any form of exercise from aerobics to yoga can act as a stress reliever. Physical exercise helps to relieve stress because it relaxes your muscles, and stimulates your brain to release hormones that increase your blood pressure and your heart rate. Being active can boost your feel-good endorphins and distract you from daily worries. (More on exercise in Chapter 10.)

Depression

Depression is a worldwide issue. According to research from the World Health Organization, an estimated 121 million people worldwide currently suffer from depression with approximately nineteen million people suffering here in America. More than 60 percent of all people who die by suicide suffer from major depression, a condition in which a person feels discouraged, sad, hopeless, unmotivated, or disinterested in life. Generally, when these feelings last for a short period, it's called "the blues" or "being down in the dumps." However, when these feelings last for more than two weeks or when the feelings interfere with daily activities—taking care of family, spending time with friends, or going to work or school—it's likely a major depressive episode.

Millions have functional depression, also known as situational depression, which is the feelings of being sad, or disheartened, on more than the occasional basis. Some of the life challenges that create functional depression include abuse, conflict, death or loss, genetics, major events, personal problems, serious illness, and substance abuse. We've all had one or two of these experiences at one time or another, but if we're not prepared to handle them, they can reoccur and eventually become major depression.

Earlier we looked at the differences in how men and women respond to emotions. There are also differences in how depression affects men and women. Approximately six million American men suffer from depression. In comparison, nearly twelve million American women suffer from depression. Women are twice as likely to develop depression as men because of the interaction between biological and cultural factors. The female endocrine system generates a number of hormones that men do not possess. Hormones, or neurotransmitters, are responsible for mood regulation. They also regulate one's appetite, sleep, and arousal. As women age, hormonal changes occur that affect behavior, mood, and physiological processes as well. When external events happen to a woman who isn't equipped to cope with these stress-inducing circumstances, these neurotransmitters may become imbalanced, causing intense or chronic depression.

Men have the tendency to feel depressed without feeling sad. They feel more anxious, frustrated, and hostile than women do when depressed. Men are also more likely to escape from depression by using alcohol or drugs rather than seeking professional help, while women are likely to seek help from friends, clergy, or professionals.

The physical symptoms are more prevalent in depressed men than women. They complain of chest pains, backaches, joint pains, and digestive issues. Psychologists attribute this to the fact that men tend to repress strong emotions rather than talk about them, unlike women who usually turn to friends or family members for support. In most cultures, men are more reluctant to ask for help, especially when it involves emotional or mental issues.

Get Help for Depression

Depression is among the most treatable of psychiatric illnesses. Between 80 and 90 percent of people with depression respond positively to treatment, and almost all patients gain some relief from their symptoms. Take a look at how Audrey was able to get relief.

Audrey had been battling with depression since she was a teenager. It began with the divorce of her parents and continued when she got involved with an older guy who was emotionally abusive to her. The impact of these experiences followed her into her adulthood, where other life events would cause cycles of depression. In an attempt to start a new life, she moved to two different cities but was extremely lonely both times because she didn't have friends. As a result her depression intensified. Then, Audrey got married and had a baby, but experienced postpartum depression. She continued to experience depression after the loss of a job, which then manifested itself as the fear of losing another job. Although she was on medication for her depression, she didn't feel that it was helping and wanted to get to the root of the cause. That is exactly what we did. Through our sessions, we were able to identify what was causing these sad emotions and feelings. By developing activities and a planned strategy, Audrey was able to reprogram and refocus her mental and emotional energy. Her positive energy translated to more energy, higher self-esteem, a new job, and a better relationship with her husband.

If you've found yourself feeling down or blue, there's a way to take control of your depression. The discussions in this section are for those of you who are not experiencing major or clinical depression. If you are at that stage of major depression, I strongly urge and advise you to seek professional help. For those of you who have found that a situation or life event had you feeling down, there is hope, because depression is tied to your emotions and feelings and you can learn to manage them. The feelings of sadness and hopelessness can be thwarted with focused integration of some suggested techniques in the road to preventing depression.

ROAD TO PREVENTING/DEALING WITH DEPRESSION

1. **Acknowledge your feelings.** Avoid suppressing your feelings. Be conscious about your feelings and emotions and admit to yourself that you're feeling sad, lonely, hopeless, etc.
2. **Understand that life events will happen to everyone.** Acknowledging this will help you avoid the lonely feelings that can overtake you when it seems that you're going through a problem that no one else understands. Know that everyone experiences problems of some sort.
3. **Allow yourself the time to "feel" the emotions.** You will be flooded with a plethora of feelings, and that's okay. You need to walk through these feelings. Don't be afraid to be angry or cry; these are natural feelings that people often try to suppress. If you are angry and need to scream, go some place where you can do that privately. When you need to cry, get it out. Don't hold back the tears. Although you may have heard or been taught that tears are a sign of weakness, they are not. They are very cleansing for the soul and body.
4. **Focus on the people or things in your life that are good.** Even in the best of times, it's good to appreciate your blessings, but it's especially imperative during difficult times that you direct

your attention into a spirit of gratitude. It doesn't matter how bad the situation is, it always could have been worse.

5. **Don't run and hide**. Your natural instinct may be to go into a shell and avoid all the people that love you. It's like saying, "It's *my* personal pain and I want to work through it alone." Tonya felt as if she didn't want to tell her friends and family about her breast cancer so they wouldn't worry about her. However, in times like these, you want to engage in the opposite thinking. The more you isolate yourself, the more prone you'll become to experiencing long-term depression. Without the support, love, and encouragement of others, it's more difficult to find your way back.

6. **Focus on, and enjoy, the present**. Challenging life situations have a way of giving us a different perspective on our journeys and almost force us to prioritize what's important. Work to enjoy the people and things that are in your life today!

7. **Volunteer your time to a charity**. This strategy is extremely helpful because it allows you to focus your energy on helping someone else. It will help you take your mind off your situation; give you something to look forward to; and help you to feel valuable. It will also give you a sense of gratitude as you deal with other people and see that your situation isn't so bad.

8. **Join a support group**. There are hundreds of different support groups available to help you deal with your challenges. Support groups provide you with an outlet to talk to and bond with others who are dealing with the same problems, emotions, and reactions. They also provide accountability for you and care about your well-being.

Your emotions and how you deal with stress are the underlying factors to your health. Learning to manage them is critical for your mind, body, and spirit. What I want you to take away from this chapter is that, again, you are in the driver's seat of your health. Becoming deliberate about how you deal with your feelings and how you regulate stressors in your life is up to you. If you want stress-free living, take the steps to make it happen. Use the roadmap exercise below to become emotionally healthy and balanced.

Roadmap

1. **Understand what you need**. Identify what you need to make your life less stressful. Maybe you need to block out negative, outside noise. If that's the case, you may need to watch less news. Maybe all of your kid's activities, and the drop-offs and pickups that go with them, are getting tiresome or overwhelming. If that's the case, work out a car-pooling schedule, or eliminate an activity.

2. **Get rid of toxic people**. Talk about stress! This tip is so important that I have dedicated the next chapter to just this topic. It will really help to change your life.

3. **Give others the benefit of the doubt**. Some of the people that upset you or stress you out are filled with tons of pains and issues. If there is someone who tends to annoy you and gets under your skin because of their attitude, personality, or actions, give them some slack. You never know what is happening in their life. Many times people are crying out for help and don't know how to get it. Do not allow them to stress you or become a problem for you. Refocus, and remember that it's not personal.

4. **Let go of the baggage from the past**. We all tend to carry things from our past that keep us from making progress into the future. Some people have huge suitcases that they are lugging around. You can get so used to carrying stuff that it becomes a part of your life and you don't really feel the heaviness. Baggage comes in the form of anger, unforgiveness, negative memories, hurt, jealousy, people, etc.

5. **Spend at least thirty minutes a day on you**. Taking time for yourself every day is critical. You need the time to get balanced, rejuvenated, centered, and to de-stress and just chill. You are sending your body signals and telling your mind that *you* are important. Your body and mind wants and craves for you to take care of it and feel good. As you may have noticed, I didn't include physical stress management techniques, because I have a whole chapter devoted to your health. Take note of other techniques in Chapter 10.

6. **Create an "Emotional Wellness Preparedness Plan."** We are good about preparing for emergencies such as fires, threats to safety, and natural disasters. There is time taken away from work and school to schedule drills to practice how you should conduct yourself in the event of an emergency. The drills take place when there is *not* an emergency and the logical part of your brain takes in the information and stores it. Should an emergency arise, the information is stored in your subconscious and can be recalled logically without your emotions taking over. But where is the emergency plan for your life? If you haven't prepared a logical plan ahead of time, like many of us, then when a situation does happen that you weren't expecting, your emotions take over and you can't think rationally. I have created an emotional preparedness plan to help you prepare for those times. If you would like a free copy, you can download one from our Web site.

EIGHT

Unwanted Passengers

*Identifying and Veering Away from People
Who Are Toxic*

I MAGINE THAT YOU have a passenger in your car who is telling you how to drive, talking loudly, changing your music, complaining about traffic, or displaying road rage. Although you have a no-food policy in your car, you notice the passenger unwrapping a burger and dropping French fries and ketchup on the seat. This passenger will inevitably get you off focus and distract, irritate, and drain you. These antics and distractions could cause you to miss your turn, become lost, or, even worse, cause an accident. Your goal is to get them out of your car as quickly as possible.

Toxic People in Life

Similarly, when it comes to your life, you don't want a toxic passenger sabotaging your journey. Toxic people come in all colors, shapes, and sizes. They are beautiful, average, unattractive, slim, medium, heavy, tall, short, ages five to ninety-five, yellow, brown, cream, white, red, black, male, female, poor, middle class, wealthy, blonde, brunette.... I think you get the picture. This means that there are no visual indicators for a toxic person; they do, however, exude negative energy and undermine your emotional wellness.

Your body and spirit will give you signs to help clue you in to who is toxic. That's right: you may have a physiological reaction to some people. When you see or talk to them, you may start to have a headache or upset stomach. Your breathing pattern may change and your heart rate may increase. These are signs that people typically ignore, but it can be harder to ignore the negative words and actions of these people.

Types of Toxic People

Perhaps you recognize some of these types of toxic people in your own life:

Complaining Charlie: *Nothing seems to ever go right for me... I can't get a break... Life is hard... Nothing is ever fair... I hate my job...*

Dramatic Doris: *You won't believe what happened now... I didn't even say anything and they started yelling... I wasn't trying to fight, they hit me first... I'm not going to let someone say that and not have something to say back...*

Gossiping Gladys: *Wait until you hear this... I heard that... Did you know that...? I just saw on Facebook that... I have something to tell you, but you can't tell anybody...*

Leaching Larry: *Can you help me fix my car? I need to borrow... Can I get a ride? Can I crash at your place?*

Hating Hazel: *You think you can do everything... That dress is not your style... You look better with longer hair... I wouldn't wear those shoes if I were you...*

Blocking Billy: *That's not going to work... When are you going to get a real job? I wouldn't start a business if I were you; I heard that 90 percent of businesses fail...*

Pitiful Polly: *I wish I were more like you... I don't have the skills you have, so no one wants to hire me... You are so pretty, you don't have the problems that I do... Life always seems to go well for you...*

Angry Andrew: *Man the world is messed up…I hate where I live, and everyone is crazy…My bosses never like me, and I don't like them either…*
I have given them names that make the descriptions humorous, but these types of people are a serious matter because of the havoc they can wreak on your life, by draining your energy and even making you physically sick.

I know from a difficult personal experience how painful toxic relationships can be.

When my family moved to Dallas for a new job opportunity, I only knew a handful of people. I immediately got involved in my kids' school and at our church, where I met many great people. In the beginning, everyone seemed so nice and friendly. I formed a friendship with a group of mothers with whom I had a lot in common: same-age children attending the same school, church affiliation, and other activities. We quickly formed a bond and had a great time as we planned birthday parties, play dates, family outings, and etc. But, sometime in the midst of all the fun, things began to change.

I first noticed that my name was no longer on the invitation list to all of the events, and I found myself on the outside, without a clue as to how I got there. I noticed that one "friend" in particular started making comments to me about the things that I was doing, my business, and my kids, saying things like, "You act as if you can do everything," and "Why do you have to be involved in so much?" She was referring to the fact that I was a business owner, choir directress, and in other leadership roles at church and at the school. I was starting to notice that whenever I got off the phone after talking to her my stomach had an empty feeling. *What's with the attitude?* I knew that I hadn't done anything to upset her. I continued to allow her in my life, ignoring what my body, mind, and spirit were telling me.

One day I called one of the "friends" in the group and I heard other familiar voices in the background. I had a strong sense that these women were talking about me. Have you ever felt that way? My advice is to *trust your instincts*. If your intuition is telling you something, believe it. I knew something was fishy and it turns out these women had gone to her house for a fundraiser that had turned into a "gossip party."

As the word began to get back to me about this "party," it confirmed what I already felt in my spirit. I was appalled to learn there were about seventeen people at this "party" at one time or another, and many hurtful and negative things were said about me that day. My so-called "friends" focused on my business, my degree, my abilities, my parenting style, my kids, etc. When I heard the things said about my children, it took me over the edge. Everyone knows that you *do not* mess with a mother bear's cubs. Feelings of hurt and betrayal consumed my thoughts. I felt like my friendship world had caved in and I had been truly stabbed in the back. After all, these people were in my circle, and I thought they cared about me, but they had turned on me. As we discussed in Chapter 6, words speak either life or death, and they just killed a friendship.

I did what I knew I had to do. I deleted every person involved out of my phone—and my life. You can imagine it was not easy. Most of us crossed paths at church, school, and in the neighborhood, so I saw them on a very regular basis. I was determined that I was going to hold my head high, not stoop to their level, and prove that I didn't need them in my life in order to live or succeed. While it was an incredibly lonely feeling, I found other ways to cope. Out of that experience, I started a nonprofit organization for women called The Six Million Dollar Woman's Club. It was an organization that focused on building women's self-esteem, knowledge, and assurance through sessions that addressed communication, health, spirituality, confidence, finances, and relationships. We also mentored women in homeless shelters and gave out scholarships to women wanting to advance their education. In the end, many women benefited as a result of my difficult experience, including me, having learned a valuable lesson about how and when to rid your life of toxic people so as to avoid tons of stress.

Getting Rid of Toxic People

As the Emotional Wellness Doctor, the one question I get asked over and over is: What do you do you when you have a toxic person in your life, especially if that person is in your family? In these next sections, I am going to give you strategies on how to get rid of (or manage, when elimination from your life is not possible) toxic people. Before getting started, let's examine your role in toxic relationships. If you are continuing to attract toxic people to you, what kind of energy are you putting out? We discussed in depth the bodies of energy in Chapter 5. For review purposes, we will look at three of the energy bodies that are attracting the people you have around you.

Emotional Energy contains the emotional patterns, feelings, and vibrations that determine your personality and also how you feel about yourself and how you interact with others. If you are constantly angry, always feel helpless, or are consistently fearful, these patterns or vibrations get locked in your emotional energy field and become a part of your personality. This determines your interaction with others and the type of people that you attract.

Mental Energy contains the structure and patterns of all the thoughts and belief systems that you consider to be true and how you react to what you think. You will have a tendency to attract people who think the same way that you do. So ask yourself, "What am I thinking about?"

Spiritual Energy contains all the information related to your experiences and reflects your consciousness of all that has been learned and experienced. It contains your higher intentions, your sense of what is right and wrong (your conscience), and your desires to increase your awareness of your purpose, place, and mission for this lifetime.

The energy that you carry and put out in these areas determines your personality, charisma, outlook, success, failure, friends, and the type of relationships in which you are involved. If you are a negative, pessimistic person who thinks the world hates you, you will probably attract like-minded people. If you are a fun-loving, outgoing, positive person, then you are going to attract that type of person. This is not to say that opposites don't attract. There is merit to that. It is possible to attract and get along with people who have different emotional energy from yours, and even different spiritual energy, but it is more difficult to get along with someone whose mental energy, thoughts, and beliefs are not the same as yours. So what type of energy are you putting out there?

Why Do We Allow Them to Stay?

When you can understand your role in your relationships, you can see that it's not one-sided. The toxic person is not just hanging on in your life. You are allowing them to be there. Here are some types of people who allow toxic people to stay:

The Rescuer: People come to you so that you can save them. You enjoy feeling like the savior, even if these people drain you emotionally, mentally, physically, and sometimes even financially.

The Problem Solver: People are attracted to you because you can solve their problems. Whatever they are dealing with, you have the answer. You enjoy the feeling you get from bringing solutions to the table, allowing them to become dependent on you instead of figuring it out for themselves.

The Parent: People are attracted to you because of your nurturing personality. Even though you are the same age as your friends, you still feel a sense of authority because you make better decisions than they do and can lead them. You enjoy feeling like the mother hen, even if they leave you with all the responsibility and truly act like children.

The Dump: People are attracted to you because you are a "great listener." You enjoy feeling like you are lending an ear, but really you feel drained because of everyone's problems clogging up your spirit.

The Rock: People are attracted to you because you are a tower of strength. It doesn't matter the problem, you never fold. You enjoy the feeling of being rock-solid and firm, even if you have to hide your emotions and pretend not to feel in order to remain strong.

Did you see yourself in any of the above examples?

REST STOP

Examine what kind of energy you are producing to keep attracting the same kind of people.

Do you have good mental, emotional, and spiritual energies? In your notebook, write down the names of the toxic people in your life and answer the following questions:

1. What are you getting out of the relationship?
2. Why are you holding on?
3. Why is it hard to let go?
4. How would your life look if they were not around?
5. Can you really change their energy?

Once you have answered those questions, you will probably notice that you are getting something out of the relationship as well. You may even fit into one of the categories I mentioned earlier. Write in your notebook if you see yourself as any of those—the Rescuer, the Problem Solver, etc. What can you do differently so you don't find yourself in that role?

How to Deal with Toxic People You Can't Avoid

In order to move forward in life you need to be prepared to cut the toxic person or people out of your life completely, just like I did with my "friends" in Dallas. However, in certain circumstances it's impossible to get rid of toxic people completely—if they happen to be coworkers, family, etc.—so you'll need strategies to minimize the impact they can have on your life. The rest of this chapter will give you strategies to either rid your life of or manage those toxic people.

Dealing with Toxicity in the Workplace

COWORKERS

Amanda dreaded going to work some days because of Ella, who always seemed to know exactly when Amanda was going to arrive every morning. As soon as Amanda got close to her cubicle, Ella would meet her with the latest gossip and negativity. Amanda would get an ear full about how their manager was incompetent and how the new receptionist acted as if she thought she was better than anyone else. By the time Amanda had gotten her coffee and fired up her computer, she was already drained. How could this one person take so much away from the day that hadn't even started?

A coworker can be difficult to deal with since you can't hit the delete key; you have to see her and work with her on a daily basis. Yet it can be incredibly difficult to deal with a colleague that causes you distress, annoys you, or undermines your work. In order to have a functional relationship with them and maintain your positivity and productivity in the workplace, use these simple strategies:

1. **Set your boundaries**. Since it's impossible for you to run away, it's important to establish your boundaries and minimize interactions. For example, you should decline invitations to join the gossipy lunch sessions with toxic colleagues or, if you're attending a meeting, sit the farthest distance away from them so their energy won't affect you.

2. **Limit your interaction time**. If it seems that they make a beeline to your desk every day so they can chit-chat, inform them that you only have two minutes to spare. Stick with that time limit and clearly communicate it.

3. **Become solution-oriented**. Instead of listening to their problems and drama for thirty minutes during your lunch break, tell them they

have five minutes to cry on your shoulder. After that, you will work with them to solve the problem. Often these people aren't interested in solutions, just venting, so this tactic will discourage them.

4. **Overshadow their negativity with positive energy.** One of the best ways to negate negative attitudes is to shower your toxic colleagues with positive words and energy. When they start talking about how terrible things are, refocus the conversation by talking about the wonderful things.

5. **Above all else, always treat them with respect.** You have to give respect to get it. Just think and remember the Golden Rule: Treat others the way you want to be treated.

BOSSES

Henry could sense that his manager questioned his competency. Although Henry knew that he was smart and able and had the résumé to prove it, his manager's sarcasm and micromanaging were beginning to make him question his own ability. His manager would consistently double his workload and demand unrealistic deadlines. When Henry couldn't manage the load, he would make it appear as if Henry was not competent. While Henry knew that his manager couldn't be classified as a nice guy, he seemed to really have it out for him. All of this stress was taking a toll on him emotionally and causing headaches and other physical symptoms.

It's even more difficult to deal with a toxic manager than with a peer. I have heard many stories like Henry's about how stressful it is to work with a toxic manager. This not only causes emotional stress but can wreak havoc on your body as well. People tend to feel like they can't do anything about this situation because of fears about job security, retaliation, or being thought of as too aggressive, confrontational, or a trouble-maker. Some managers seem to thrive on making others miserable and are angry, unhappy, lacking in leadership and social skills, tyrannical, controlling, overbearing, a perfectionist, and/or a workaholic. Just understand *they* have the issue and not you. Although they may bring issues and stress to you, you don't have to internalize it. Since you can't remove them from your space, you have to learn coping skills that will keep you emotionally healthy. Henry followed these next steps in order to deal with his manager. They can help you too:

1. **Remember, it's not personal.** Many times in these situations, you are not alone. Know and understand that your awful boss is likely making everyone's life miserable. This should help you to know that it is not about you.

2. **Give managers the benefit of the doubt.** You never know what they're dealing with in their personal or professional lives. They may be getting pressure from their boss(es) and aren't sure how to handle it so they pass it on to others. Make a decision that you will not take on what may be their personal problems.

3. **Communicate your concerns respectfully.** When given the opportunity—for example, during evaluations or open-door meetings, or even by scheduling a meeting with your supervisor—gently and respectfully share your concerns. Some people are not aware that their behavior causes stress for others, and they may never know because no one is assertive enough to share.

4. **Communicate your work boundaries.** It is your job to take care of you. While this may be a delicate area, I would encourage you to affirm and communicate your work boundaries: how long you can work overtime, how late you will answer emails, etc. I suggest this for two reasons. One, it will help you feel that you have some level of control over your life. Two, it will help ensure that you maintain a good work/life balance as much as possible, so you don't find yourself working until 8:00 p.m. every night.

5. **Put the ball in your manager's court.** Oftentimes managers may be unaware of how heavy your workload is. You can communicate that to them via email by writing, "I have projects A, B, C, and D that are marked urgent; what would you like me to focus on?" Knowing exactly what to prioritize will help mitigate the stress of trying to get everything done all at once.

6. **Show respect.** It is of utmost importance to always show your manager respect, even in spite of his or her actions. Again, the Golden Rule always applies: Treat others the way you want to be treated.

7. **Change jobs.** This is the last resort and only if you have the opportunity and your job is making you physically sick. Always keep your résumé up to date and ready to be distributed.

The reality is that we will all deal with a difficult boss or toxic coworker at one point or another, so it's vital that you learn effective strategies to deal with this situation. The important detail to remember is that you are in the driver's seat and can determine how you deal with these people. Using the strategies that I have outlined will help you to increase the level of power that you have over your life while decreasing the stress.

Dealing with a Toxic Family

You didn't choose your family and they didn't choose you. You just get what you get. While that is duly noted, what happens if your family is crazy? I definitely ask that affectionately, because we all have family members that we can classify as "crazy." The process for dealing with family members becomes extremely delicate because they are with you for life, like it or not. Be it a difficult relationship with a parent, sibling, or child (I will cover all three), the best way to decrease stress is to learn how to manage your relationships with family members by making sure you are in the driver's seat.

PARENTS

It was difficult for Grace to hold back the tears as she shared with me the power that her father had over her life. As an alcoholic, her dad was very difficult to live with. He was filled with anger, and made Grace feel like she was nothing. His mistreatment of her mother weighed heavily on Grace as she grew into a young lady who became the caregiver in her parents' home. Her mother had become codependent, so Grace felt like she was in charge through much of her childhood. Although her dad eventually left her mother, he continued to reappear in Grace's life, making her feel obligated to give him money and stirring up negativity among her siblings. She wanted to rid her life of the negative energy, painful memories of her childhood, and the constant turmoil that her father still brought to the family.

Perhaps you can identify with Grace's story. I certainly can from my own complex relationship with an absent father. It's incredibly challenging to have a parent who makes you sick, weighs you down, drains your energy, causes drama and stress in your life, steals your dreams, etc. When this is the case, you must understand that your parent has his or her own set of issues that they are projecting on you. It's hard not to think of it as personal, because sometimes it is. Maybe you remind them so much of the other parent with whom they have conflict. You know the comments: "You are just like your no-good daddy," or "It's too bad that you are so much like your mother." In those instances, they have anger and unresolved issues that they may take out on you. Just remember it is still *their* issue. Bottom line is, whatever the source of conflict you have with your parents, you can employ these strategies to help you carve out a relationship that works for you.

1. **Do not internalize their issue**. You must avoid feeling in any way responsible or guilty in terms of your parents' issues and challenges. You did not cause them. You also don't want to take on the emotions they project on to you. Just because they may be angry, spiteful, or morose doesn't mean you should too.

2. **Don't feel that you can fix them**. It's natural to feel like you can fix your parent(s). As you get older and wiser it can become a goal of yours or even your mission in life. However, you must not get wrapped up in their lives; it will definitely affect you, your immediate family, and your health. They may need professional help, and you can't give that to them.

3. **Set your boundaries**. It's important that you set some time limits as well as other guidelines that will help you manage your life. If your

mother calls with drama, wanting to talk to you for hours, you will need to say gently yet firmly that you love her, but you only have fifteen minutes, or whatever your limit is, to talk. In addition, if your parent drops by for unannounced visits and brings issues and drama to your household every time, you'll need to set limits that will work for you and your family.

4. **Don't allow them to drain your energy.** You're in charge of your space and time. If things are going well, but take a sudden turn down drama lane, it's okay to shut down the conversation gently. You can say, "I don't want to talk about that," and then change the subject.

5. **Avoid feeding the negative.** Avoid getting caught up with the negative conversations by adding your own negative two cents. Try to refocus the conversation to something positive.

6. **Communicate your feelings with respect.** Regardless of how dysfunctional your parents may be they still deserve your respect. You have no right to yell, curse, or treat them badly because of how they may treat you. Treat them like you want to be treated.

7. **Distance yourself until you heal.** In some cases, the only answer is distance. You need to give yourself time and space to heal. If that is something you need to do, make it a point to communicate this with your parent(s) in writing. You can email, text, or send a letter. This respectful behavior lets them know that you are alive, and are healing, and it will help them to maybe do the same.

SIBLINGS

Hazel's brother Rick was one of her biggest life challenges. She was older than he was and always took her big sister role seriously. When he lost his first job, she agreed to let him come and stay with her for a while. She soon realized that he wasn't really trying to find a new job. She felt like she couldn't put him out since he was family. He had no money, so he wasn't helping with the bills and he would consistently ask her for money. He always had relationship drama and unloaded his problems on her, hoping that she could help him work them out. She cried out to me for help and felt like she couldn't endure another minute of this stress. I helped her integrate the strategies to manage their relationship. She is less stressed and has ceased to be an enabler.

We have all heard of or may have experienced sibling rivalry. While this is a natural part of life, some of the issues and challenges that siblings face growing up never go away. I have talked to many clients who have bad blood between them and their siblings. Having grown up with sisters and being the youngest, I know firsthand the competition, jealously, arguments, etc., that arise. Some sibling discord is expected and normal, but when there are intense anger, jealousy, drama, and fights even after becoming adults, then the relationship can be classified as toxic. So what can you do?

1. **Understand the origin of your issue**. Sit down and evaluate: Where did the issue with your sibling start? Many times the problems started so early on in your childhood that you don't even know exactly what happened or why you don't get along. If you can identify the root, it is easier getting rid of it.

2. **Discuss and apologize for past behavior**. What you should realize is that many things that happened when you were kids were not intentionally malicious. Some things were taken out of context and some behaviors could just be chalked up to immaturity. Explain your side of the story, listen to your sibling's side of the story, apologize, hug, and move on.

3. **Let it go**. Don't keep bringing things back up with the trips down memory lane. Even if you don't get a chance to have a discussion, you are in control of you, and you still need to let it go. Holding onto hurts of the past will cause emotional stress, physical stress, and cloudy futures.

4. **Create new rules of engagement**. If you are able to have a sit-down meeting to address the past, it is good to come up with new rules of engagement for the future. That means discussing what your relationship will look like moving forward.

5. **Grow up**. Now that you are older, it's time to grow up. You can't stay trapped in the behaviors and dynamics from your childhood. You are not ten years old anymore; you are an adult, so act like it.

6. **Show respect**. Even if you decide that you really don't like your siblings or their actions, and don't want to be around them, still show them respect. Avoid talking about them with other family members, friends, and parents. At the end of the day, they are still family.

7. **Distance yourself until you heal**. With any relationship that cannot be repaired, sometimes you have to let them go mentally. This may mean that you have to distance yourself from interaction with your siblings. You can send Christmas cards, birthday cards, and acknowledgement of other significant days without having interaction. I never suggest living life as if they don't exist. They are family and rest assured that one day a life event will bring you together.

CHILDREN

Cora's son had seemed troubled from the time he was eight. His school years were peppered with truancies, detentions, parent conferences, and even a misdemeanor. As an adult, he never seemed to find his way. Cora tried to help him as much as she could. He couldn't keep a job, so she was always giving him money. He constantly cried to her that he felt like a failure, but he didn't seem to try very hard to get his life on track. Although he was twenty-nine, Cora didn't have the guts to put him out. But she despised coming home from work and sitting on the couch with his girlfriend watching TV for the night. She thought it was the last straw when she found out that his girlfriend was pregnant, but she still couldn't put him out. She was caught in a cycle and didn't know how to stop it.

I believe that a toxic child is by far the most difficult toxic person to deal with. As a parent, it's so hard to comprehend that the sweet little baby you once held in your arms and cuddled could be poisonous to you later on in life. As a mother of four, I know that each child comes with a different blueprint, personality, and energy. As parents, we do all that we can to ensure that our kids are healthy and happy. Some children can have a predisposition to anger, negativity, risky behavior, stubbornness, etc. Throughout their developmental and adolescent stages, they can actually seem to (and some do) "lose their mind." If you have found that your child is stressing you to abnormal limits—you are crying at night, constantly upset, on edge, sick, scared, or they are a financial drain—this child has become toxic to you. While you love your children unconditionally, it is important to realize that you can't make them do what **you** want them to. Although it is easier said than done, this is when you tell yourself not to stress over things or people you can't control. I have listed steps for dealing with a toxic child.

1. **Don't take it personally.** What is happening with your child is usually not about you. It is some personal issue that he or she is dealing with but will displace the anger to you and those that love him or her. In some cases, however, the issue *could* be you. If that is the case, I recommend seeking professional counseling.

2. **Lose the guilt.** Although as parents we seem to have an endless capacity for guilt, we are not responsible for the choices and decisions that our children make. They have their own lives to live and they have to make their own choices. Encourage yourself by knowing that you did the best you could and the future is about their choices.

3. **Show tough love.** If your child is repeatedly in trouble, using drugs, or making other bad choices, it is important for you not to enable his or her behavior by authoritatively laying down rules and guidelines.

4. **Don't add fuel to the fire.** Avoid confrontations, fights, and using words to discipline them that may add fuel to the fire. For example, when you say something like, "Over and over again, I've tried to tell you not to do that and you just don't seem to get it," their interpretation is, *My mother thinks I am stupid*, which can make them feel even angrier and more isolated.

5. **Let them go.** If your children are grown and have moved out of your house, you have to get to a place where you can let them go.

That means, again, understanding that they have their own journeys and will be creating their own paths in life. Sometimes what is required is for them to know that you as their parent have totally put the ball in their court.

6. **Know that you can't fix them.** It is natural to want to fix your kids. As a parent that is what we do—fix their problems. You won't be able to fix your child. I would suggest that you get them professional help.

7. **Support them, not the bad behavior.** There is a distinct difference. Love and support them through their wrong choices, addictions, and hurts, but make it very clear that you do not support the choices or the addiction itself. They need to understand that you love them but not what they're doing.

Dealing with your family can be extremely difficult. The dysfunction that I see in families can be overwhelming. Again, the key is to understand that you are only in control of your own behavior and reactions, not anyone else's. Work to become the family member that is the change agent. You can influence your family with positive energy. While it may not be easy to do, don't give up. At the end of the day, family is the backbone to our society.

Dealing with Toxic Friends and Lovers

FRIENDS

Friends are the easiest to remove from your space when it comes to getting rid of someone toxic. After all, they are in your life only because you have *chosen* them to be there. You can also choose for them not to be there. In friendships, there is always a possibility for issues to arise and for people and events to influence your relationship. Sometimes, just through the evolution of time and changes, you can naturally grow apart. But what happens when they evolve into someone who is toxic? It can become difficult to let them go because of your emotional ties, history, commonalities, and memories. It is still important to break that bond.

Olivia was a different person from the girl with the ponytails whom Juliet had grown up with. These days, Olivia always seemed negative and talked badly about other people. All she did was complain about her family, her job, and her relationships. She would typically call Juliet, talk to her for an hour, and never once ask about Juliet's life. When Juliet would attempt to sneak in something that she wanted to talk about, Olivia would take over by saying, "That same thing happened to me." Juliet was tired of listening to all of her whining and complaining. They had known each other for twenty years and she felt like she was Olivia's only friend. She also felt that Olivia was sucking the life out of her, but she didn't know how to distance herself without hurting her feelings.

Then, Juliet used the following strategies and has been able to distance herself without totally cutting off the friendship. These steps include a gradual progression of moving them out of your space once you have established that there is not equal value in this friendship.

1. **Establish your boundaries**. Know what you will and will not accept. If you don't want to be contacted after 10:00 p.m., then make that very clear. Remember, you have to teach people how to treat you.

2. **Communicate your concerns**. Have a conversation with your friend to let him or her know your thoughts about the friendship. In all fairness, ask your friend for his or her input as well, but let him or her know that you are not willing to continue the friendship under the current conditions.

3. **Stop feeding them**. What that means is that you are providing them something that causes them to want to keep coming back to you. Stop enabling their behaviors.

4. **Be solution oriented**. Instead of listening to the problems and drama for thirty minutes, tell them they have five minutes to cry on your shoulder. After that you will work with them to solve the problem. You will be amazed how that will cause them to run

away. Since they thrive on drama, they aren't trying to solve their problems, so that will also cause a natural deterioration of the relationship.

5. **Cut them off.** Okay, sometimes in certain relationships you just have to cut them off. I would always advise having a conversation first, if possible. On a few occasions, it may be better to send an email or a letter if you can't have a face-to-face conversation. That is not to advocate breaking up a friendship in a cowardly way, but sometimes if there are a lot of emotions involved, a conversation could lead to a lot of hurtful words—just something else you would need to heal from. I do recommend some form of communication since it is healthy to have closure. Then you can do as I did: hit the delete key in your mind (and cell phone) and keep it moving.

LOVERS

As with toxic friends, getting rid of a lover can be very painful. Although a lover is not a family member, getting rid of one can be equally as complex because of the emotional, physical, and spiritual ties, as well as the possibility of children being involved. Before we go into how to clean your space, let's look at the two types of toxic lovers.

1. **The Drama Drainer:** This is the person who doesn't add anything to your life but takes it all away. Drama Drainers are constantly filled with—what else?—drama and keep your life on edge. Although they drain your mind, body, and spirit, you keep them around either because you think you can fix them or because you find the one good thing about them and justify their existence in your life. Everyone around you knows that they are no good for you, but you ignore your loving family and friends because of that "thing." You know they are holding you back, but you can't seem to let them go.

2. **Subtle or Overt Abuser:** This is the person who continues to mistreat you, disrespects you, drowns your dreams, ignores you,

or abuses you physically,* mentally, or emotionally. Emotional abuse can be any type of mistreatment that occurs that makes you feel less than, unequal, invisible, isolated, neglected, exploited, alone, etc. Emotional abuse is rampant and yet it is the least discussed form of abuse because of the blurry lines that define it. It can include very subtle behaviors, thereby making it difficult to solidify and prove. The shape of emotional abuse takes on many forms. It can be the silent treatment, simply ignoring or failing to acknowledge your presence, or making hurtful comments. It can even be controlling behaviors like withholding money.

Does either of those scenarios sound familiar to you? If so, you need to take steps to change your situation. The lingering impact of not doing so is tremendous. It is like a drip of water that will gradually corrode rock. It chips away gradually at your self-esteem so that many times you aren't aware that it's happening until one day you wake up and say, "Hey, I don't feel alive." If you're in a relationship that's toxic, especially if it has escalated to physical abuse, then it's time to take these actions:

1. **Love yourself.** You have to love yourself more than anything. These kinds of toxic relationships will make you question and second guess who you are. Spend time with yourself and get to know you again. Love the person you see.
2. **Set your boundaries**. Declare that you will not tolerate certain behaviors anymore, from the present person or anyone in your future.
3. **Establish your game plan**. Breakups are things that should be thought through and planned out. Because it is filled with so

---

* If you are being physically abused—pushed, poked, pinched, hit, slapped, tripped, threatened, or tortured—I encourage you to leave the relationship as quickly as possible. If it has happened once, it will happen again. Your health, self-esteem, image, energy, and life are in danger. There is never a reason for your partner to put his or her hands on you in anger. If you need help immediately, call the national abuse hotline: 1-800-799-SAFE (7233).

many emotions, it is imperative that you plan on how to handle certain pieces and situations that may arise. For a relationship breakup plan go to www.creatingamazinglives.com.

4. **Communicate your intentions**. Proclaim your goal that you need to break off this relationship while communicating your boundaries.

5. **Cut them off.** You have to let them go. You can't allow the back-and-forth conversations, episodes, intimate liaisons, etc. Although it is hard, you have to cut them completely out.

6. **Stick with the plan.** No matter how hard they try and pull at your emotional heartstrings, don't allow yourself to be lured back into the trap. Put on your running shoes and don't slow down until you are far removed.

7. **Seek healing**. In an abusive relationship, it is very important that you seek professional help of some kind. In these types of relationships, there is a lot of emotional and spiritual damage that has been done and you will need to talk to someone to help you sort through your feelings.

8. **Surround yourself with love and support**. During a tumultuous time it is ideal to indulge in the relationships that give you support and love. These relationships will help to build your self-esteem as you work your way back to loving yourself.

9. **Feed your spirit**. Keep your spirits high, by reading, mediating, praying, and listening to positive music.

Roadmap

There are so many tips and strategies given in this chapter, that this roadmap looks a little different. It is a simple thought, however, and it will help you have a more positive journey:

Surround Yourself with Beautiful People—If you think about a bouquet of flowers, each flower is unique with different petals, scents, and colors.

Each delicate flower is arranged to make a beautiful bouquet. When one flower starts to wilt, it affects the whole bouquet. So you discard the one flower so you can still enjoy the beauty of the others. You must keep it watered so the flowers will last. When the flowers are old and start to die, the water that once kept them alive will start to stink.

Think of your life as a bouquet and the people in your life as the flowers that make up your life. All are unique and colorful in their own way. Relationships that start out beautifully sometimes start to wilt. Just like the bouquet, if you let people who have withered stay around, they can affect your life and how it looks. If they hang around long enough, things began to stink.

NINE

Who's Riding Shotgun?

Solidifying Your Relationships

I F YOU WERE GOING to drive 3,000 miles across the country, who would you want in your passenger seat? The person who popped into your mind is more than likely someone that you love and trust, and someone who you get along and have fun with. That person is a very significant factor in your overall well-being. You feel that this person supports you and you can be yourself when they're around. If you're married or have a significant other and you didn't choose that person to be your road companion, you may want to think about why you didn't choose them. It may be a sign that you feel something is missing in your relationship. Maybe you don't have fun or get along with them. Perhaps you can't be yourself when you're with them.

The passenger that you choose will make the difference in the following:

- How far you travel
- Where you go
- How many stops you make
- How much you enjoy the trip
- The memories you create along the way

This is analogous to your life. Who is the person or people in your life that you are carrying along on your journey? Is your relationship with your significant other helping or hindering you along the way?

The people that you are in a relationship with can enhance or interfere with your life. Having a relationship is about how you feel and behave toward someone.

I have talked with thousands of people—at my speaking engagements, counseling sessions, and life-coaching sessions—who have shared with me countless stories, issues, and lessons about how they relate to others. In this chapter, my goal is to help you to understand relationships from the psychological perspective. I also hope that you will have a clearer picture about why we do some of the things we do in regard to relating to others.

In my experiences with people, and consistent with research conducted by the American Psychological Association (APA), two of the top five reasons for stress are relationships and finances. Think about this for a moment: stress is one of the main reasons that people fight, kill, are imprisoned, fall from leadership positions, commit crimes, make regrettable decisions, etc.

There have been thousands of books, millions of blog posts and articles, conferences, radio shows, talk shows, and public and private conversations that have discussed relationships, yet so many people are still struggling with them and relationships are failing every day. As an expert in human behavior, I want to help you understand the male and female psyche, which will help you manage your relationships. The goal of this chapter is to help you see relationships differently and implement some strategies that will affect your and others' behaviors. Let's start at the basics and explore human needs.

Our Needs

Basic Human Needs

I remember being an eager freshman student in Psychology 101, learning all about Sigmund Freud, Maslow's Hierarchy of Needs, and Ivan Pavlov's dogs. At just eighteen years old, I had no idea that the material I was learning about had become an introduction to my life's passion, or that I would dedicate my life to helping people understand their own behavior.

One of the first things you learn as a psych student is Maslow's Hierarchy of Needs. This is a psychological theory proposed by Abraham Maslow concerning human motivation. He believed that individuals possess a set of motivation systems unrelated to rewards or unconscious desires. The model first included five basic needs to which he later expanded the model to include cognitive, aesthetic, and transcendence needs. The expanded model is listed as follows:

1. **Biological and Physiological needs**: air, food, drink, shelter, warmth, sex, sleep, etc.
2. **Safety needs**: protection from elements, security, order, law, limits, stability, etc.
3. **Belongingness and Love needs**: work group, family, affection, relationships, etc.
4. **Esteem needs**: self-esteem, achievement, mastery, independence, status, dominance, prestige, managerial responsibility, etc.
5. **Cognitive needs**: knowledge, meaning, etc.
6. **Aesthetic needs**: appreciation and search for beauty, balance, form, etc.
7. **Self-Actualization needs**: realization of personal potential, self-fulfillment, and personal growth and peak experiences.
8. **Transcendence needs**: helping others to achieve self-actualization.

Having an understanding of our physiological and psychological needs helps to lay the foundation for our other needs. Each one of these needs is interdependent and builds on the others. For example, your physiological needs have to be met before you can focus on fulfilling the need to belong, etc. The basis for this is helping you to see that your significant other will not be able to focus on your relationship if he or she is struggling with safety or esteem needs. There are also additional fundamental needs that I would like to present. These needs have been summed up based on my experiences in working with people over the last two decades. I have categorized them as emotional needs.

Human Emotional Needs

1. **Need to be heard.** Everyone wants to be listened to and feel that people will pay attention to what he or she says.
2. **Need to be validated.** Feeling validated is the next level after being heard. It is critical that someone not only hears what you say, but confirms that they have listened and understood your opinions and ideas.
3. **Need to feel important.** Each person has a need to feel worthy of consideration or would like to feel that he or she has considerable influence or authority.
4. **Need to be valued.** It's important to feel that you are highly regarded by others and have worth. There is a need to feel valued by others in your workplace, church, organizations, families, and definitely in your personal relationships.
5. **Need for attention.** Your first loud cry was heard as you made your grand entrance into the world. It was the first cry for attention and it hasn't stopped. Many things that people buy, wear, drive, etc., are designed so that they can be noticed. If good attention is not rendered, people will resort to getting bad attention to fill the need.
6. **Need to be missed.** How many times have you asked or have been asked by someone, "Did you miss me?" We all want to know that the absence of our presence will bring sorrow or regret to others.

Each of these needs serve to bolster your self-esteem. Having your emotional needs met confirms that you are important and that you are worthy to someone. If you could keep this list of needs in mind as you relate to your partner, it would help to resolve many communication issues. We will stop for a moment and see where you are with respect to meeting your partner's needs.

REST STOP

It's notebook and evaluation time. First, write down the six emotional needs that we reviewed. Writing them down will help to imprint them into your mind. We all need to: be heard, feel validated, feel valued, feel important, receive attention, and be missed. Answer the following questions with regards to your partner:

1. Do you listen to your companion?	Yes	No
2. Do you validate him/her?	Yes	No
3. Do you value him/her?	Yes	No
4. Do you make him/her feel important?	Yes	No
5. Do you pay him/her focused attention?	Yes	No
6. Do you let your partner know you miss him/her?	Yes	No

If you answered no to any of these questions, it may explain conflict or distance in your relationship. This will also help you to know the behaviors that you need to enhance to elevate your relationships.

Distinctive Behaviors of Men and Women

The main reason why relationships are difficult, and why there are so many misunderstandings, is the simple fact that men and women differ mentally. It all starts with the wiring of the brain. In the early chapters, I discussed some of the differences in how emotions and stress affect men vs. women; however, there are other differences causing certain behaviors that are worth noting. These four categories explain the differences in how the brain perceives, interprets, and responds for men and women:

1. **Communication:** Women have a tendency to communicate more effectively than men. Women will talk through issues and

utilize nonverbal cues such as tone, emotion, and empathy. Men tend to be more task-oriented, less talkative, and more isolated. Men have a more difficult time understanding emotions that are not explicitly verbalized, while women tend to intuit emotions and emotional cues. This is because women's brains tend to employ both sides to process information, while men's brains tend to rely primarily on their dominant or language side to process. The dominant hemisphere tends to be analytical, problem solving, task-oriented, detailed, and verbal, which helps to explain common male behavior.

2. **Thinking:** Men tend to process information better in the left hemisphere of the brain, while women tend to process equally well between the two hemispheres. This difference explains why men are generally stronger with left-brain activities, such as problem solving from a task-oriented perspective, while women typically solve problems more creatively.

3. **Language:** The two sections of the brain responsible for language are larger in women than men, which is one of the reasons why women excel in language-based subjects and in language-associated thinking. Men typically process language in their dominant hemisphere, whereas women process language in both hemispheres.

4. **Pain:** Men and women perceive pain differently. Women are more likely to vocalize their pain and to seek treatment for their pain than men. The amygdala is activated when one experiences pain; for men, the right side of the amygdala, which is associated with external functions, is activated; for women, the left side of the amygdala, which is associated with internal functions and lends itself to feelings of intensity, is activated.

There are more detailed books written about the human brain and its functionality. There are also more detailed comparisons of the brain in different sexes, but for our purposes, these points are the most significant. Now that you have some background on the science of relationships, this should help you in relating to, communicating with, and understanding your partner. So much of what men and women do can't be helped, so you should be sensitive to certain needs. When someone says, "I can't help it, I am just made that way," it *is* true.

The Needs of a Woman

Okay, so I have heard countless men repeatedly tell how complicated women *appear* to be. There is merit in that notion since there are many intricacies and delicacies to a woman. When something is complex, it warrants your time and attention to study, figure it out, and draw conclusions. To help simplify things, I have put together a list of the seven core needs of women from my own quantitative and qualitative research:

1. **Security/Stability**: In the relationship, as well as financially and physically
2. **Affection/Intimacy**: Closeness not necessarily involving sex
3. **Communication/Conversation**: To be talked to and listened to
4. **Praise/Compliments**: That involves abilities, body style, clothing, and general appearance
5. **Honesty/Openness:** Sincerity and genuine actions and words
6. **Commitment/Loyalty**: Fidelity and monogamy
7. **Attention/To be desired**: Notice the details, emotionally and physically

The Needs of a Man

When it comes to men, we have heard the exact opposite: They are simple. Simple in needs, desires, and wants. And, from my own interviews, research, and experiences, I can substantiate that claim. Let's look at the list for men:

1. **Respect/Admiration**: For who they are and what they do
2. **Sex/Play**: That involves desire and creative energy frequently
3. **Food/Cook**: Fix a great meal, curb the hunger
4. **Support/Encouragement**: Their jobs, dreams, hobbies, friends
5. **To be needed/Feel necessary**: Feel they are a necessary addition to your life

REST STOP

It's time to evaluate and find out where things are in your relationship.

Rate your satisfaction level on a scale of 1–10 (low–high):										
Communication	1	2	3	4	5	6	7	8	9	10
Respect	1	2	3	4	5	6	7	8	9	10
Support	1	2	3	4	5	6	7	8	9	10
Sex/Intimacy	1	2	3	4	5	6	7	8	9	10
Security/Stability	1	2	3	4	5	6	7	8	9	10

What are the areas that you feel need improving and why? The point of this exercise is to evaluate and see where you are in your relationship. I want you to think about the things you used to do that made your relationship fun and that can enhance these areas. Have your partner evaluate the relationship as well. See how his or her answers compare to yours. Share your ideas about enhancing your relationship with each other.

ROAD TO COHESIVENESS

1. **Understand and appreciate the differences in each other.** Knowing that there are scientifically proven mental and emotional differences between men and women should help you in your relationship. Avoid being mad because of the differences. Embrace them and let them help to balance you.
2. **Learn the communication style of your partner.** While there are gender differences, there are also personality differences that determine how we think, react, and process information. If you would like to take a simple personality test that will help

you learn about your partner, go to our Web site www.creating amazinglives.com and download the test. It will really help you to understand how to deal with each other.

3. **Take time to evaluate your relationship periodically.** It's essential to the success of your relationship. Use the simple chart in the activity section that was presented to evaluate where things are every three to six months.

4. **Create a game plan for your relationship.** You have to discuss what will work for each person to get you back on track. Create an actual plan that you write out for each person to see and have a copy. It will help keep you on track.

5. **Work to satisfy the needs of one another.** Once you determine what is lacking, a conscientious effort and hard work will be required to fulfill the needs of each other. If you put in the work, your relationship will grow in a positive direction.

Just Go With It (JGWI)

Listed below are things I call "Just Go With It" (JGWI) factors. There are a few things about each gender that you may never understand or "get." Don't waste time or energy trying to figure them out. Just know that because of the differences that we have covered above, each gender has its own way of functioning. It may not make sense to you, but JGWI.

FOR MEN
1. **Conversations women may have with you and/or girlfriends.** It may seem that women talk in circles to you and to each other. That's because the communication style of women is like a chain-linked fence. Thoughts and words become linked together. You may start out talking about her day at the office and the next minute, she is talking about her aunt at the family reunion. JGWI—something you said triggered that transition.

2. **Shopping.** Many women like to shop for themselves, their kids, their pets, etc. You may wonder how someone could spend all day shopping (or browsing) or how they could feel excited about the bargains that were garnered on the excursion. And the age-old question: Why so many shoes? JGWI.

3. **Emotional actions/responses.** As I have explained in earlier chapters, women respond differently than men when it comes to many of life's events. Coupled with the difference in the brain and body, it's difficult to predict what is happening inside of a woman. With the combination of hormones that can run wild and the brain processing thoughts and information, try not to take it personally if you get an unexpected response.

FOR WOMEN

1. **Sports.** The fact is that the majority of men love to watch all types of sports activities. Sometimes it doesn't matter what kind; if it's on the competitive field, it qualifies as a "sport." During the games, they become emotional—they scream, yell, laugh, get angry, dance, and sometimes cry. Don't question—JGWI. Learn to enjoy some sports to spend more time together.

2. **Withdrawal.** Men don't process issues like women. Their tendency is to close off the rest of the world, which includes you, and think through what they need to do. If they can't find refuge in their home, they may seek it outside of the home. Let them have their space. Don't insist that they talk things out with you when they are in this place. They will come around.

3. **Emotional response/reaction.** As I have explained in earlier chapters, men respond differently than women when it comes to many of life's events. Coupled with the differences in the brain and body, what is a big deal for you may not be for them. Their ability to let go of emotional events/information is really a plus for women. It can also provide a good balance.

Why Relationships Break Down

We are constantly bombarded with the dismal statistics that remind us that approximately 45 percent to 50 percent of first marriages end in divorce. Second marriages end in divorce 60 percent to 67 percent of the time and third marriages fail 70 percent to 73 percent of the time. There is no way to measure just how many cohabitating, committed and semi-committed, relationships end daily. There are many reasons as to why couples divorce or break up, including disagreements about finances, bad communication, sexual issues, infidelity, differences in parenting style and religion, and addiction or abuse. While this is not new information, I would like to offer what is underneath many of these issues. But first I want to talk about how most relationships start.

1. **The honeymoon phase**. You new partner is sexy and hot; he or she makes you laugh, is sensitive, smart, understanding, financially stable, progressive, etc. Let me give you insight on what is actually happening in your brain when you feel these early butterflies.
    - *Male: Testosterone.* Hormones are high with the thrill of the chase and the attempt to win a partner over. This raises his testosterone level and makes him feel a sense of strength and confidence. He will be more energetic and more affectionate or attentive.
    - *Female: Oxytocin.* During the honeymoon phase a woman's hormones are high as she feels protected, provided for, and loved. This raises her oxytocin level and makes her feel more affectionate. She may also experience more energy, joy, and be more carefree. Be aware during this stage. As a woman, you are responding and making decisions that will affect your relationship based on emotions and feelings and not logic.
2. **The real person appears**. Now reality sets in, your hormones have settled, and you actually see that this person has faults. You knew they were there before, but those hormones were swirling in your brain and masking the obvious. You partner isn't so perfect after all. Now what? It is during this time that faults can

seem huge and you begin to wonder how you missed them. You may even feel like you have been duped, tricked, or that your partner was not honest with you about who he or she is.

3. **Reassess to see if you really like this person.** You can now see faults, some of which you may begin to despise. Your partner's defects can begin to overtake his or her good qualities.

4. **Irritation and annoyance sets in.** Now you are irritated because you don't like what you see and you are easily annoyed at the things that your partner does or doesn't do.

5. **Communication issues exist in abundance. It's hard to talk to someone when you are irritated or annoyed with them. Arguments begin to increase** as you don't see eye to eye anymore.

While this a typical cycle, it's not to indicate that all relationships go down a path that leads to their demise. The relationships that make it through are those that decide they are willing to and do accept the faults of each other. This behavior cycle ensues for the couples whose relationship breaks down.

Pain: A BIG factor in the Breakdown of Relationship

What actually lies underneath the way we behave and respond to others can be summed up in one word: **pain.**

In Chapter 3, I talked about how insecurity is the one roadblock that we all have to overcome. However, even underneath the insecurity, there is usually pain. Some type of pain caused you to become insecure. There is no getting around pain. It is a part of life. It can be physical or emotional. Physical discomfort can be caused through violence, injury, or illness. Emotional pain is a mental suffering. I mentioned briefly in Chapter 6 that "hurt people hurt people." This is generally what happens in relationships that breakdown. We all begin to experience physical and emotional pain very early in life. If I asked you to recall the first time you remember falling or having a bad experience at school or at home, you could vividly recall the situation. If the pain is physical, your body knows how to heal itself. If your pain is emotional, there is no guide as to what you should do. You are given advice from those around you who don't know what to do with their pain either. Some common advice include, "You need to get over it," "You have to move on," "Don't let it get you down," "Things will get better," "Don't think about it," "Try and forget about it," "Don't let it take over your life," etc. While those statements may sound positive, people are generally not equipped to tell you how to move on or get over it. Since no one ever teaches you to heal from pain, you either suppress it or store it in your subconscious. Thus, we all bring stored-up pain to relationships.

Types of Pain

There is a litany of pain that has been racked up by the time you enter into a relationship, some of which includes:

- Words that have cut and bruised your spirit
- Bullying
- Mistreatment from others
- Betrayal
- Lies
- Abuse
- Abandonment

These are just a few of the things that possibly caused you pain somewhere in your life. Because you have stored your pain, you carry it into your relationship. Both parties may come with pain that has not healed. Behaviors are triggered when someone does or says something that reminds you of a past pain, which causes you to lash out, say hurtful things to each other, plot revenge, or run away. Think about it.

The reasons that I previously listed for divorce and break ups included finances, communication, sexual issues, infidelity, parenting style, religion, addiction, and abuse. For each of these reasons, if you dig deep enough, there was more than likely some pain that was not dealt with that caused certain behaviors. Take Mia's case.

Mia grew up with a controlling father. His dominant and aggressive personality made her develop into a quiet person who was rather passive. When she met Collin, he was mild-mannered and their personalities seem to gel. He helped to bring her out of her shell because he made her feel comfortable. Things were fine while they were dating. It wasn't until after they got married that she started to notice that Collin was becoming more dominant. When he began to ask a ton of questions after she arrived home from having dinner with her friends, she started to shut down and withdraw into her shell. A flood of memories of the pain from her childhood caused her to withdraw from him. His intent wasn't to hurt her, but he didn't know the extent of her pain.

How to React to Pain

Concerning what we do with pain, I heard one explanation in a sermon from Pastor Conway Edwards at One Community Church in Allen, Texas. He said there are three ways we can deal with pain:

1. **Medicate it.** Use drugs, alcohol, food, shopping, gambling, or other addictions to dull or mask the pain.
2. **Be motivated by it.** Pour your pain into your work, projects, goals, and getting things accomplished.
3. **Meditate on it.** Think about your pain while it continues to brew. You usually will plan some sort of attack or revenge.

Which way do you deal with your pain?

REST STOP

What are the hurts and pain that you have stored from your past? Briefly write down any pain that you have encountered from your past relating to your:

- Childhood
- Parents
- Siblings
- Friends
- Relationships

This exercise will help you to acknowledge the pain, which is the first step to healing. You can begin a process of categorizing and walking through the pain, which will take some commitment and work. I have listed some steps to help you move toward healing and recovery.

ROAD TO RECOVERY FROM PAIN

1. **Acknowledge your pain.** The first step in any recovery process is to acknowledge that something exists. You have and feel pain, so admit it and accept that it is there. You may have tried to repress it and forget about it so it will go away, but I encourage you to embrace it.
2. **Acknowledge your emotions.** Write down in your notebook how the person or the event related to the pain made you feel. Be honest with all of your feelings. If you are angry and filled with contempt, put that down. This will help you to release some of the feelings.

3. **Decide that you want to release the pain.** As discussed in Chapter 2, you have to make a clear declaration to your mind and body that you want to release the pain. By making that decision, you are saying that this person or situation will not have power over you any longer.

4. **Write a letter to the person.** One of the best healing mechanisms is to write a letter to the person who has hurt you. Express your thoughts and feelings and the pain you have experienced. Writing a letter is helpful even if you can sit and have a conversation with the person; it will help you to be organized in your thoughts and not get too emotional.

5. **Send, or dispose of, the letter.** You have to decide if it's valuable to send the letter to the person or people who hurt you or if you need to dispose of it in some way—tear it up, burn it, or flush it. Sometimes, in some situations, it's important to have a conversation with the person who has hurt you. This can only be done and be beneficial to you if you are in a place where you can articulate your feelings without anger.

6. **Let it go.** You are consciously choosing to give up your role as a victim. This is a process that requires you to create your own closure. It will require that you block the negative thoughts and the incident when it comes back to your mind. Replace it with words of affirmation. In Chapter 12, I talk about how to forgive, which is a process of letting go.

7. **Seek professional help.** I will continue to advocate professional counseling in these steps. Sometimes that is the only thing that can get you through some of the hurts from the past.

8. **Turn the pain into something positive.** Some of the most positive things and organizations have been created out of pain. In Chapter 8, I shared my experience of starting a nonprofit organization because of my pain.

Learning how to manage and heal from your pain will be a huge step in transforming your relationships. Start to live in consciousness about the things you do and say and why you do or say them. If you can understand and control your own behavior, half of your battles are over.

What Makes Relationships Successful

We have reviewed basic needs and talked about gender differences in brain processing, as well as the emotional needs of each gender, so now let's look at what makes relationships work. Before I do that, keep in mind that no relationship is perfect. Everyone has his or her issues, problems, disagreements, and headaches. The key is that you should have an understanding with each other as to what works for your relationship, not anyone else's. When all is said and done, we all want successful and solid relationships.

Here are ten tips and strategies that will help guide you to creating a healthy relationship.

1. Set Boundaries and Guidelines for Your Relationship

It is important to talk about boundaries and guidelines at the beginning of a relationship. However, it's never too late to have the discussion. Remember to be realistic. Many times, we think that we can or can't handle certain things such as betrayal, mistrust, and infidelity. Talk about these sensitive issues before they happen. Ask questions like:

- What do you want your relationship to look like?
- What works for your relationships?
- What do you like? What don't you appreciate?
- What will you tolerate?

Boundaries need to be addressed within your relationship, as well as with outside interactions or distractions such as: cell phones, interactions with colleagues and friends of the opposite sex, chat rooms, etc., I also believe it *is* critical to discuss social media, as it has become one of the newest forms of interaction that causes problems in relationships. I will talk about Facebook in particular, as it has been documented as partial reasons for divorce. According to a report by Divorce Online, a third of all divorce filings in 2011 contained the word "Facebook." And more than 80 percent of U.S. divorce attorneys say social networking in divorce proceedings is on the rise, according to the American Academy of Matrimonial Lawyers. Because it and other social media sites are affecting people's relationships, I feel that it is important to include this section about Facebook.

FACEBOOK

A. **Set relationship boundaries for FB.** Assuming that you already have a Facebook account, if you have not done so, stop and schedule time to sit down and talk with your partner about the expectations and the rules of the game that work for your relationship. You will need to decide how you are going to handle accepting friends, posts, pokes, relationship status, photos, and other personal things. You will need to discuss how much of your personal business you want to reveal online for the entire world to see. It's human nature to wait until there is an issue and then intervene. You can avoid so many arguments and conversations before they happen by being upfront with your feelings and expectations.

B. **Know and understand that your partner will be connecting with old friends.** Okay, let this one soak in. The whole purpose of Facebook is social networking, which means connecting with people. Yes, there will be blasts from the past. That long-lost flame that once had the heart of your sweetheart is more than likely one of the one billion plus people who use Facebook. He or she is out there and may want to reconnect with your partner, so be realistic about it. So that this does not catch you off guard, prepare for it and expect that it will happen. The key is not allowing it to become an issue in your relationship. How is that done? Talk about it before it happens. You may be thinking, *That's not going to happen! I have never really talked about my ex to my partner because he or she can't handle it.* Or, *What's in the past is in the past.* Well, the moment that you *reconnect* with a person, he or she becomes a part of your present. It's difficult to compete with the past and the memories that are stored in your heart, so it can be a difficult conversation to have. However, since we are talking about how to have a solid relationship, this is something that you must deal with or it will be an issue.

C. **Don't allow FB to control you.** According to *Business Insider*, Americans now spend roughly 16 percent of their total online time on Facebook. To break it down even further, *Mashable*, a social media news outlet, reports that the average U.S. user spends about eight hours a month on Facebook. That is equivalent to spending one full workday a month just browsing one Web site. Sure, it's easy to get caught up in all the information, feeds, videos, posts, birthdays, links, apps, games, photos, etc. We also know that there are people that easily spend a few hours a *day* on Facebook. There are some people who are always on Facebook no matter what time of the day or night that I log in. I have wondered, *"Do they have a life?"* The many hours spent on Facebook can have a negative impact on your relationships. Limit your time and your connections.

2. You Have to Have a Plan

Creating a plan, arrangement, or strategy for your relationship isn't something that people generally think about. But you must decide how you want your relationship to work. For instance, if you have agreed that you will check in with each other at least twice a day, the plan can be: let's touch base once before noon and again by 10:00 p.m. This helps to establish expectations so that you aren't arguing because someone called you twice before ten o'clock in the morning, but then you didn't hear from him or her for the rest of the day or until he or she got home.

3. You Have to Be on the Same Page

It is critical that you maintain unity and agree on your vision, goals, and values. Disharmony takes place when you don't share similar points of view in those categories. This is not to say you have to agree on everything, but you do need to be able to agree to disagree. You also may have a different way of achieving certain goals, but as long as you agree on the goal itself and the end result, you will be okay.

4. Learn to Listen to Each Other

I have heard that women speak more words than men. I have seen studies that claim differences in men and women's speech as much as men using 7,000 to 15,000 words and women 20,000 to 30,000 words per day. While that is interesting and makes for good conversation, researchers at the University of Arizona conducted an eight-year study and found that women spoke an average of 16,215 words a day, while men spoke an average of 15,669. That's not a huge difference, so what is the all the chatter about?

The issues are not related to how much men and women speak, but rather their different communication styles and listening abilities. As mentioned earlier in the chapter, men and women not only communicate differently but they also process the information they hear differently. For these reasons, you must learn to listen to the other person.

5. Manage Your Emotions

I spent an entire chapter on emotions because they are so important and can make or break a relationship. Learn to experience your emotions without letting them get in the way. Remember, you can't think logically and emotionally at the same time. Pipe down, chill out, and take a deep breath. It's going to be okay.

6. Manage Your Expectations

This is huge. The majority of the time when you have issues in your relationship, it is about unmet expectations. The cycle happens as follows: You have a silent expectation that your partner doesn't know about. Your expectation wasn't acknowledged or met, so you become hurt or angry, and an argument ensues. Your partner is clueless as to what you are even arguing about. This incites you even more because you feel he or she should have known (i.e., read your mind).

For example, you are excited about some news that you have received. You share it with your mate and their response is not as excited as you want or think (read: expect) that it should be. You become hurt and upset, because your mate doesn't seem as happy as you are. They are unaware that this news is a big deal. Your feelings take over and you now have shifted into a funk. You are not even happy about the news anymore because of the unmet expectation of a response.

Here's a simple technique to prevent that scenario. Say the following to your partner: "I am giving you some exciting news and I hope you are going to be excited too." That helps set your expectations and for the two of you to get on the same page before you share the news. In many cases, you should sit down and have a conversation about expectations to make sure you are in the "real" zone.

A. **Don't project your thoughts and feelings on someone else.** Just because you may feel insecure does not mean you should put the responsibility to reassure you on another person. For example, it's your spouse's class reunion and he doesn't want to attend. You were looking forward to going so everyone can see who snagged the hunk from high school. You are immediately upset because you can't imagine why he wouldn't want to go and think he may have something to hide. Instead of saying gently, "I was really looking forward to attending your class reunion," you immediately jump to other conclusions: maybe he isn't proud of you or maybe the ex will be there and there are still unresolved feelings. You provoke an argument based on your insecurities when all the while he had an entirely different reason for not wanting to go. This confrontation could be avoided if you asked your partner about his thoughts and feelings rather than indulge your own insecurities.

B. **You don't have to say everything you think.** Learn when to speak and when to be quiet. The perception is that women have a greater tendency than men to say what is on their mind. I used to think that I needed to say everything. Even though our ego tells us that what we have to say is important, and that others *need* to hear it, I have learned that some things are better left unsaid and there is great benefit to practicing the art of silence.

C. **Maintain simplicity.** The synonyms for "simple" are: easy, straight-forward, uncomplicated, trouble-free, effortless, and unfussy. Those words sound wonderful when it comes to thinking about your relationship, but are they possible to achieve? I believe so, but it requires conscious effort. We are all guilty of causing a firestorm by fanning a small flame. Really, is it a big deal that the toilet paper is placed on the roll a certain way or that the bed was half made? Life is too short. Don't sweat the small stuff.

D. **Enjoy the moments you have together.** Do you find that you are either spending your time arguing about the past or worrying about the future? Stop! Take it one step at a time. What are your plans for the present? How will you make each other happy today? Focus on what you can do to make your partner smile today.

The Business of Relationships

Be prepared, because it's time to challenge you to think outside the box. I don't know if you have heard the saying that a relationship is a full-time job, but there is truth to that. Let's compare your relationship to working for a company. The purpose of this mental exercise is twofold.

First, it's to let you see that typically you give more thought, time, and energy to your employer than you do your relationship. You give the best of what you have to the people who don't really matter in the grand scheme of things. Sure, you have to do great work to keep your job, but transfer that thinking over to your relationship as well. You have to do great work to keep the person you love. And second, this exercise lets you think differently about your relationship. In a relationship, you really have entered into a commitment with another person that you are where you want to be and you want to do your best to stay there. Isn't that the same way you think about your job? Whether you are an entrepreneur or an employee, you have to put your best foot forward to be successful. Do the same for your relationship. Read over the comparisons. It is food for thought.

Research

Company—Investigate the company that you are interested in working for to check out its history, future plans, skill level needed, pay scale, and job benefits.

Relationship—Investigate the man or woman that you have an interest in dating. This can include looking at online profiles and receiving referrals from friends who can give you the scoop on his or her history, interests, skill level, financial values, and benefits.

Interview

Company—You show your interest by sending in a résumé. You are granted the interview and you know that you have to put your best foot forward to sell yourself. The first impression will make all the difference in the world. Appearance is important so you put on your best suit and look classy from head to toe. The interview process is usually scary and can be intimidating. Your job is to sell yourself and your skills and to convince the company of your value. At the end of the interview, you usually know if you would like to work there, so you either hope that the company hires you or you delete it from your list.

Relationships—You display your interest by initiating or accepting a date. Appearance is important so you put on your best outfit and you look good from head to toe. Dating can be scary, but you put your best face forward. You feel that you have to sell yourself and convince your date of the value you could add to his or her life. At the end of the date, you know if you would like a second date or if you want to cross him or her off your list.

Hired! (Novice)

Company—You sold it, and now you are hired. You are excited, motivated, and committed to give the company your all. You know that you have to go through hands-on training and you are eager to learn and please. You work hard to show your immediate value. You come in early and leave late. You volunteer for projects and are determined to learn all you can. You attend all office functions, understanding your presence is a plus.

Relationships—You sold him or her, and now you are in a relationship. You are excited, motivated, and committed to give your all. You are eager to learn and please the other person. You work to show that you are the only person for him or her. You plan and schedule events and spend time together, understanding the importance of getting to know each other even better.

Veteran

Company—You have settled quite nicely into your company. You know your way around and now others call on you for your expertise. You are reliable, loyal, and dedicated. You continue to come to work early and sometimes leave late. You have become a leader among your peers as your set your sights on a promotion. You can't afford to slack off knowing the opportunities for the future. You are not necessarily looking for more responsibility, but definitely more money and perks. A great title never hurt anyone either!

Relationships—You have settled in. The excitement has waned. You know your partner quite well and there are no more pretenses. But here something starts to shift. Instead of continuing to put your best foot forward, your appearance is not so important. You are comfortable and slack off on some of the extras that you used to do. Instead of looking ahead and working for your relationship elevation, you focus more on the past, pain, memories, and become complacent.

As you can see, the similarities between working at a company and being in a relationship are striking. I want you to continue on the track of the company. You will find that if you stayed with the mentality that you have at work, your relationship would be more fulfilling.

Company Guidelines for Your Relationship

1. There is a proper way that you can communicate your concerns to your boss, employees, or peers. It is done with respect and an awareness of everyone's feelings.
2. There is a process for complaints.
3. There is a process to evaluate you and your overall performance.
4. Self-evaluations and personal and professional growth plans are encouraged.
5. If there are issues, you can be placed on an improvement plan before being fired.
6. Everyone works for growth, development, and to be promoted.
7. Team building exercises and activities are planned.

Look at your relationship and implement these company guidelines into your relationship dealings. Know and understand that good relationships require work, dedication, patience, and commitment. Avoid giving all your best to your job; leave some energy and smiles for the person you love and have committed your life to. You may find yourself guilty of giving your best to others, and giving your family your leftovers.

Roadmap

1. **Know that you are not alone.** Everyone has problems and nobody's relationship is perfect. Where there are people, there are problems.

2. **Admit that your relationship needs help.** You instinctively know that your relationship is not what you want it to be, but you have to admit it to yourself and your mate to get the help you need. Confide in trusted friends, a pastor, rabbi, priest, or a counselor to help you find your way. Don't get caught up in thinking that you can find your way by yourself.

3. **Change lanes.** Sometimes you are just driving in the wrong lane in your relationship. Get out of the fast lane. You may be creating stress for each other. Slow your pace and start taking time for one another. Set up date nights and short trips. Alone time is important. Slow down and take some things off your plate so this can happen.

4. **Get to the nearest rest area.** Occasionally, you need to stop and rest. The fast pace of life and the need for urgency in accomplishing things causes unsettled spirits, sleep deprivation, and health problems, which can create arguments and disrupt the peace. Sometimes it's important to take a break from each other. It's essential that you spend alone time to renew and rejuvenate yourself.

5. **Recalculate your route.** When you discover that your relationship is headed in the wrong direction, stop and recalculate. This includes that evaluation process that will let you know just where you are. Plan what you need to do differently in order to get you headed in the right direction. What is significant to note here is that there is more than one way to reach a destination. If the road you are traveling on is too bumpy, has too much traffic, or construction, you have to reroute.

6. **Learn how to manage conflict.** Just in case you didn't know, there is no such thing as a conflict-free relationship. It will find you. The couples that are the happiest have learned how to minimize and manage their conflict. Below are some steps to help you manage your conflict.

   a) **Know that conflict is inevitable.** You are two individuals with different thoughts, values, and opinions. Conflict doesn't have to be negative. It's just something that happens when two people don't agree.

   b) **Think before you speak.** Watch your words. What you say is so important. Try to refrain from talking too much when you are angry. Once the word is out, there are no take-backs. The words used in anger are often the ones that stick and you regret.

   c) **Your partner is not the enemy.** You are not fighting a war with each other, so calm down. Ask yourself, is it really that deep?

   d) **You don't always have to be right.** That's the truth. Being right is not always what is important. We spend so much energy trying to prove a point, but at the end of day, peace is what should prevail.

The last tip that I want to leave with you is, *act like you want to be treated.* Implementing that tip in your relationship alone will do wonders. It will help to monitor the many feelings and emotions that can turn negative; enhance communication skills; and keep your thoughts and actions positive.

TEN

Time for a Tune Up!

Treating Yourself Right—the Mind/Body Connection

H AVE YOU EVER PURCHASED a new car—perhaps your dream machine—from the showroom floor? Think about that car. It came to the dealership directly from the factory with everything brand-spanking new and operating perfectly, from the internal components to the interior gadgets. And now it's yours! In the glove compartment, the owner's manual tells you everything you need to do to keep it working properly. For maximum performance, it's essential that you take your car in for regular maintenance, oil changes, tire rotations, etc. To keep it sparkling and shiny, you'll need to regularly wash, wax, and buff it. Even if you keep the outside looking great, if you neglect the small maintenance needs and checkups, problems will begin to accumulate and over time, create a huge issue.

Like this car, your body is your personal machine to care for, appreciate, and keep in good, working order. You have been given total control and responsibility of this amazing machine. You are in control of the quantity and quality of the food that you put in your body, how much you rest and sleep, and how much you exercise. This is important, because as with a car, the human body will start to break down—physically, mentally, and/or emotionally—when you don't take care of it. But unlike a car that you can replace for a newer model when it falls apart, your body is your body for life, so of course you want to take very good care of it. How well are you doing in caring for and appreciating the body you have?

You may not have come with an owner's manual hidden in one of your compartments, but family members, friends, doctors, books, and many helpful Web sites are all valuable resources that will help you learn how to take care of your health. I, too, have some insight to offer you in this regard. In this chapter we will focus on tips, strategies, and recommendations for the best care for your body.

Weight and Health

First off, let's consider how much you weigh. Everyone hates the dreaded scale, but the numbers really do matter. Excess body weight can have a profound negative impact on your health and body. Breast cancer, coronary heart disease, type II diabetes, sleep apnea, gallbladder disease, osteoarthritis, colon cancer, strokes, and hypertension are all often associated with being overweight or obese. Moreover:

- Obesity is the number two cause of preventable death in the United States.
- 60 percent of all Americans have at least one chronic health condition.
- 7 out of 10 deaths among Americans each year are from chronic diseases.

So you see, being overweight is, excuse the pun, a big deal. Being very overweight—obese—is an even bigger deal.

If you're overweight, you're not alone. The statistics for obesity across the globe are staggering. Recent reports by the Centers for Disease Control and Prevention state that more than one billion people world-wide are obese. In the United States alone, approximately fifty-eight million to sixty million people are overweight, forty million are obese, and three million are morbidly obese. From the sixty million people who are overweight, nine million of those are nineteen years of age and younger, the CDC report states. As the obesity rate continues to rise, researchers predict that at the current rates, approximately 75 percent of Americans could be overweight/obese by 2020.

Did You Know?

Researchers from the London School of Hygiene and Tropical Medicine report that while the United States makes up 5 percent of the global population, Americans account for more than one-third of the world's global weight.

These statistics illustrate that we do indeed have an obesity epidemic in this country. While these statistics might be overwhelming, the good news is that we are very much in the driver's seat when it comes to choices that we make about our health and bodies. Your body is your responsibility, and you have a say about whether you become obese, or whether you lose weight so you no longer are obese or overweight. I don't believe that people *want* to be unhealthy, or that they even realize that they are deliberately making themselves sick with the choices of food they eat or a lifestyle that is too inactive. I *do* believe that we have become accustomed to immediate gratification, without a thought of future consequences.

The Weight-Loss Battle

Of the millions of Americans who would classify themselves as overweight, a huge percentage are caught in a diet yo-yo, having dieted in the past, usually multiple times, but then gained it all back—and sometimes even gained more back, and therefore planned to diet again in the future. Billions of dollars are spent each year to battle the bulge.

A glance at some of the facts of the weight-loss industry gathered by Marketdata Enterprises should help you understand the economy of this battle:

- $20 billion in annual revenue of the U.S. weight-loss industry alone, including diet books, drugs, and weight-loss surgeries; the number increases to $60.9 billion in the U.S. weight-loss market when you include programs, weight-loss chains, pills, juicers, diets, etc.
- 108 million people are currently on weight-loss diets in the United States—with dieters typically making four to five attempts per year.

You may be asking, "If there are so many people dieting and billions of dollars spent toward fighting this battle, why are the obesity and health-related numbers continuing to climb?" That is a good question. It's clearly a battle we're spending a lot of money on but not winning. In fact, we're failing. So who or what is to blame? Although there are environmental, cultural, and biological indicators that play a role in this epidemic, the majority of weight issues correlate directly with your decisions. But if you want to lose weight—and keep it off—it's going to take more than deciding to go on a diet. We see from the weight-loss numbers that spending money on trying to lose weight isn't usually enough to see lasting change. Like so much of life, bringing about a transformation in your life—such as becoming "unlost" in health matters—begins with the mind.

The Mind/Body Connection

As I have shared throughout the book, success in any endeavor starts with your mind. Gaining or losing weight is due to actions, which first began as thoughts. For example, there are things that you tell yourself to rationalize your actions:

I deserve it. I work hard and deserve to be able to eat what, when, where, and how I want.

It makes me feel good. Food makes me feel wonderful. It gives me energy and when I eat certain kinds of food, it makes me happy.

I like myself just as I am. I may be overweight, but I look great anyway. Therefore, I am going to eat what I want because I feel good about me.

It's in the genes. It's a family thing. I inherited these thick thighs and large posterior. It does not matter what I eat, I was destined to be big. And I'm not as big as some members of my family...

I can't help it. It doesn't matter what I eat. I just look at food and I gain weight.

I have tried everything. I have been on every diet in the world and still can't lose the weight, so why keep trying? I'm accepting that this is just who I am.

It's too much work. Trying to watch what I eat is too much work. I have too many other things to keep up with rather than counting calories.

I'm too busy. I don't have time to focus on my health with all the things I have to do.

I'm not disciplined enough. I need someone to help me and I don't have a trainer or a partner to work out with me.

It's too expensive to eat healthy. I can't afford to shop for healthy food or pay for a gym membership. When I get some money, I will start.

Pounds just come with age. The older you get, the more your metabolism slows down, so it's not my fault. It is a part of aging.

I'm going to die anyway. We are all going to die from something someday. I might as well enjoy my food and die happy.

Do any of those sound familiar? Or perhaps it's the procrastination bug that bites and you think, *I'll start tomorrow*, or *It's the holidays, I'll start in January*, or *When life is not so stressful, then I'll slim down.*

If one in three adults are obese, chances are that you have heard or used these excuses at one point or another. These thought patterns will sabotage you at every turn. All of these thoughts have power, and soon these "excuses" result in bad habits that inflict unintentional abuse on your body and lack of maintenance for it.

Although we tend not to classify over-eating as an addiction like cigarette smoking or drug abuse, in many ways it is very similar. It's just that stopping the addiction requires different methods. After all, we must have food to survive, so it's impossible for food addicts to go "cold turkey"! (Although we can declare "no-go" zones on desserts, salty snacks, sodas, and other especially addictive foods.) But the first step is controlling your mind, not what you put in your hands. The key is to understand how to get out of the negative cycle of thinking and change your mind about your health.

A Wake-Up Call for Victoria

Victoria had been battling with her weight for as long as she could remember. She grew up in a house where food was plentiful. Her parents were overweight and believed that people should be able to enjoy food. In high school and college, her weight didn't hinder her from having friends. Everyone knew and loved her for who she was. As an adult, she had grown to accept her weight as a part of who she was and thought there wasn't anything she could do about it. Her philosophy was she loved herself and being overweight runs in her family.

But then one day she had a wake-up call after a doctor visit and she learned that she had high blood pressure, diabetes, and the beginning or clogged arteries. Victoria first had to process that the diagnosis she received was potentially life threatening. The thought of her shortening her own life because of her food choices helped her realize that she needed to take action. She started with a plan and modified her diet. Exercise was not a part of her lifestyle prior to her doctor visit, but it definitely became a part of her plan. She committed to a minimum of thirty minutes of exercise four days a week. Through her readjusted thoughts and actions, she has lost fifty pounds in less than six months.

Jeff was tired of looking at his belly. While he and his buddies, all laughed off their midsections and justified them with age and beer, he just didn't feel as good about himself as he used to. It was only five years ago that he was wearing his shirts proudly tucked in his pants, and now that was not an option that enters his mind. He disliked having to buy pants that were bigger in the waist, but didn't quite fit elsewhere, just to provide space for his midsection. Jeff said that something clicked for him when he bumped into an old buddy of his that he hadn't seen for several years. Steve looked the same as he did in college, slender and fit: however, Steve had to look twice to recognize Jeff. Jeff said Steve joked about how he was running from old age, but it seems as if it was catching up to Jeff. Although Jeff had learned to laugh at the weight jokes, this one was different coming from Steve who was still fit. Jeff's competitive nature kicked in and he told Steve, "The next time you see me I will be twenty pounds lighter." They agreed to meet up in three months.

Jeff's determination propelled him to cut out carbohydrates and alcoholic beverages and begin an exercise program that he ordered from an infomercial. Within the ninety days, Jeff had lost five inches from his waist and toned his body. You can imagine what the meeting was like when he saw Steve again. His weight loss all began with a thought and a decision.

The Secret to Weight Loss

It appears that everyone is looking for that one *magic* pill that you swallow and the pounds melt away. And some companies try to tell you that the magic pill exists. There are some weight loss commercials that claim that by simply taking a pill or drinking a juice you lose weight, without even having to exercise or change your diet. Don't believe it. There is every kind of procedure and strategy imaginable to attempt to melt, freeze, shake, wrap, burn, suck, and pinch away the pounds, but you can't get something without doing the work. So why do we fall for these gimmicks? Are we really that naïve? Are we lazy, unwilling to do any work or make an effort?

We live in a nation of instant gratification. Losing a pound a week is realistic, but we want to lose ten pounds in a week, or in a day! But the "right now" concept is dangerous for your health. We buy into the lie that if we can't have it immediately, we shouldn't bother with it at all. It's too hard, it takes too long.

In Chapter 2, we discussed the concept of making decisions that lead to success. This approach is particularly important when it comes to making healthy lifestyle choices. You have to establish in your mind that you *are* going to lose weight—even if it takes several months—and that you will do it because you're going to be disciplined. You're going to regularly exercise and you're going to eat healthy by selecting healthy food at each meal and cutting back on portion sizes. Your very decision to lose weight will make you become intrinsically motivated to achieve your goal. When you really decide that you are going to make it happen, it is not about other people. It doesn't matter what your husband, wife, girlfriend, boyfriend, kids, friends, family, or any other people think about you. It only matters what *you* think about you. It is about you and your future. Remember, when you truly make a decision, your mind, body, and spirit will rally around you to make it happen the way you want it to.

Are you ready to make that change? This is usually one of the more difficult decisions to make and really stick to because people like to eat. Deciding that you are ready to change your health and lose weight is a commitment to change your lifestyle. In your notebook, write your answers to the following questions:

- Are you ready to commit to losing weight and taking control of your health?
- What is the reason that you want to lose the weight?
- What do you feel that you will gain from losing weight?

Emotional Eating

I would say that at least 95 percent of all the clients that I have worked with, male and female, are wrestling with weight loss. After addressing their current state of being, food can generally be traced back to an emotion/feeling of some kind. This is why once you have made a decision to change your health, it's essential that you address one of the major underlining causes of weight gain—emotional eating. If you can understand and break the cycle of food being tied to your emotions, coupled with the suggested plan in this chapter, you are on your way to a healthier life.

Overeating is often triggered by stress. The stress you felt because of the crazy day at the office or the horrific traffic you encountered on the way home can trigger a desire to eat certain types of food, usually high-calorie options—fat, sugar, and salt. According to Dr. David Kessler, former dean of Yale's medical school and FDA commissioner, "Highly palatable foods—those containing fat, sugar and salt—stimulate the brain to release dopamine, the neurotransmitter associated with the pleasure center. To de-stress, people will often grab that bag of chocolate chip cookies, or a bowl of ice cream to make them 'feel' better. Then they rationalize with a combination of the excuses discussed earlier, often 'I deserve it, it makes me happy, and it tastes good.'"

So how do you break that cycle?

A Seven-Step Plan to Overcoming Emotional Eating

1. **Admit that certain foods you eat have feelings associated with them**. First you have to come to grips with the reality that certain foods make you feel a certain way and you are responding to that; admit that you are in fact sometimes an emotional eater.

2. **Identify your feelings**. You must recognize the emotions that you feel when you eat certain foods. For instance, fill in the blanks of this sentence. When I eat _____, I feel _____, because _____. For example, "When I eat Hot Tamales (my personal comfort food), I feel happy because they taste great and connect me to my past." Make your list and complete the sentences for all the comfort foods that you eat. What you will find is that you have the same exact feelings brought on by several foods.

3. **Understand your personal history with the food**. In order to understand some of your emotions, you may need to consider the history behind the food. In other words, what were the circumstances surrounding your first consumption of or early exposure to the food? As mentioned earlier, many comfort foods can make you feel nostalgic. So think about what the history is of your comfort food and what good memories are triggered. For me, I started eating Hot Tamales when I was a little girl. My mother got paid once a month and she would give me and my sisters 25 cents to go to Woolworth and get penny candy. I know I'm dating myself with this story, but at that time you could actually get 25 pieces of candy for 25 cents. And now, all these years later, every time I enjoy these candies, I have warm feelings from childhood.

4. **Replace food with something comparable**. The reason that you are eating the food is to capture the emotion/feeling that the food is bringing about. So think about what other activities makes you happy, peaceful, calm, or content. With what can you replace your apple pie or ice cream? Also, among the food choices you've listed that bring you pleasure, choose the healthiest one and allow yourself that as an occasional treat rather than the others since they bring about the same emotion.

5. **Practice**. You have to really work to integrate your new way of thinking and being into your lifestyle. Just as with learning how to play a new instrument, you have to think about it positively,

read, and practice as much as you can to get better. The great thing about training yourself is, once you learn it and it becomes a part of you, something less than that no longer feels natural. You've trained yourself in a new way. It also helps if you practice stress-relieving techniques mentioned in Chapter 7; that way you don't overeat to relieve your stress.

6. **Recruit an accountability partner.** One of the keys to motivation is to have accountability for your actions. People have greater success when they can find a partner to work out with or there is a group of people all focused on the same goal who hold each other accountable for their actions or lack thereof. Know up front that you will slip every now and then. Don't beat yourself up. It happens to all of us. Just recommit yourself to your goals as soon as you can and have your accountability partner help you stay on task.

7. **Create a positive success plan.** Life is about plans. They are a great tool to keep you focused and accountable. This is your success plan and it has to have a positive spin. This is necessary because there are so many negative psychological barriers associated with health and weight. So it is very important to use mind techniques that will help you reach your goal. Since this is something new that you are implementing in your life and your schedule, you have to make room for it. Below are the steps in creating your positive success plan. Use the following sentence below as it is listed at the beginning of the plan. You will be amazed as to what it will do for your mind.

Positive Success Plan

My body is the ultimate interior and exterior structure.
1. I want to free myself of _____ lbs. (weight goal)
2. I will eat vegetables, fruits, proteins, _____, _____ (name specifics in the blanks) to give my body maximum health and energy.

3. I will free myself of sugar, carbohydrates, and carbonation that diminishes my health.
4. I understand that I can reach my goal faster if I commit to eating before 8:00 p.m. and refrain from indulging on evening and late-night foods.
5. Eating breakfast is a requirement to be as healthy as I can and to free myself of extra pounds. Not only does it kick-start my energy after fasting all night, it increases my metabolic (calorie burning) rate.
6. I will do structured physical activity, _____ (specify the activity here), for forty minutes a day at least four times a week (e.g., exercise routine, zumba, walking, running, Wii workouts).
7. I will focus not on what I am losing with this plan but on what I am *gaining*:
   a. Good healthy heart
   b. Lower cholesterol
   c. Lower blood pressure
   d. Lower blood-sugar levels
   e. Increased life expectancy
   f. Increased energy
   g. Increased self-esteem/image
   h. Increased positive outlook on life
   i. A great-looking body

Food for Thought

You have made a commitment and examined your emotional eating habits. I have given you a plan that will help you to understand your behavior and how you respond to food. Your mind is made up and your body is waiting for marching orders on how you need to get it done.

Say to yourself every day that you want to live each day as healthy as possible. Now of course, that is going to require effort on your part. Since we have been discussing the food that you eat, I want to share some additional health tips that you can easily integrate into your life for healthier living.

Healthy Lifestyle Choices

Add Supplements to Your Diet

Maybe you grew up, like me, with the bottle of Flintstone vitamins on the table. Ever since I can remember, I had to take extra supplements. My mother believed in the power of the vitamins. And it worked, because we weren't sick much as kids. As an adult, I continued the practice of taking vitamins and supplements. This is important because even though our bodies are these incredible machines that pull nutrients from the foods we eat, sometimes there is a lack of or an imbalance of a particular enzyme, cell, bacteria, iron, etc. Supplements help to add what is lacking.

The value of supplements was solidified in my mind as I witnessed the health challenges of my middle daughter, Jazzy. After she had a negative experience with antibiotics, which killed the good bacteria in her system, an allergist found that the lining of her intestine had been stripped of the lactobacillus in the intestine and weakened her immune system. She had to take probiotics to rebalance her body. Probiotics help in two ways. First, they help the digestive tract to balance the good and bad bacteria. The digestive tract needs to be healthy, because it filters out and eliminates things that can damage it, such as harmful bacteria, toxins, chemicals, and other waste products. Second, they help the immune system. Jazzy's digestive and immune systems had been severely compromised, so I sought out probiotics. I found a product called Florify, a probiotic produced by a company called Melaleuca. Within a week of starting her on the product, she began to tell me that she was feeling better and not experiencing stomach issues like before. I began to see an improvement in her health. I was so excited that I began to sell the product (more on that in the financial chapter). Although I am no longer working with the company, it is a product that I still highly recommend; go to www. creatingamazinglives.com for more information.

Probiotics are just one kind of supplement, but there are many types available; supplements help add to and replenish our bodies with missing nutrients. I suggest using ones with the most natural ingredients. I believe that God placed everything we need to restore our bodies on this planet; we shouldn't have to use synthetics.

It's Time to See the Doctor!

In the introduction of this chapter, I talked about your body as a machine. In fact, it is an amazing machine—but it still needs your tender loving care. The sad truth is that most people take better care of their cars than their bodies. Your car requires maintenance that includes oil changes, tire rotations, alignments, tune-ups, brake pad replacements, etc. If something isn't working right, you take your car in as soon as possible so the problem doesn't worsen and add up to more problems and money. It would be great if we treated our bodies the same, but we often don't because people don't like going to the doctor. But think about it. Your body deserves more maintenance than your car. This is your body for life. Make sure you schedule yearly wellness exams. For women, depending on your age, this includes yearly mammograms. As with your car, there are specific things that need to be tuned up, and it is important to know your numbers—blood pressure, cholesterol, heart rate, and blood sugar levels.

In addition to prevention, you need to go when you feel pain or sense that your body is out of alignment. Getting immediate help for your pain will also help you avoid bigger health problems down the road, which could otherwise add up to more money spent taking care of them. Routine doctor visits have saved many lives. Make a commitment now that you will schedule your wellness exam within the next two weeks.

Get More Sleep

You have heard from the time that you were a toddler that you need to get a good night's rest. But do you get it? Few people admit to getting the proper amount of sleep. According to the Centers for Disease Control (CDC), more than forty million workers get fewer than six hours of sleep per night—that's about 30 percent of the country's civilian workforce.

The lack of sleep can cause many problems. It can make you irritable, foggy, and lethargic. If you're feeling that way when you're driving, it can lead to accidents. In fact, the same CDC study revealed that an estimated 20 percent of vehicle crashes are linked to drowsy driving.

There are many other negative effects that occur over time from getting less than seven hours of sleep.

1. **Impaired thinking.** Sleep plays a critical role in thinking and learning. Lack of sleep hurts these cognitive processes in many ways. First, it impairs attention, alertness, concentration, reasoning, and problem solving. This makes it more difficult to learn efficiently. Second, during the night, various sleep cycles play a role in "consolidating" memories in the mind. If you don't get enough sleep, you won't be able to remember what you learned and experienced during the day.

2. **Serious health problems.** Not getting the necessary amount of sleep can put you at risk for other serious health problems, including heart disease, heart attack, heart failure, irregular heartbeat, high blood pressure, stroke, and diabetes. According to some estimates, 90 percent of people with insomnia—a sleep disorder characterized by trouble falling and staying asleep— also have another health condition.

3. **Decreased sex drive.** Sleep specialists say that sleep-deprived men and women report lower libidos and less interest in sex. Depleted energy, sleepiness, and increased tension may be largely to blame. For men with sleep apnea, a respiratory problem that interrupts sleep, another factor may play into the sexual slump: lowered testosterone. A study published in the *Journal of Clinical Endocrinology & Metabolism* in 2002 suggests that many men with sleep apnea also have low testosterone levels. In the study, nearly half of the men who suffered from severe sleep apnea also secreted abnormally low levels of testosterone during the night.

4. **Depression.** Over time, lack of sleep and sleep disorders can contribute to the symptoms of depression. In a Sleep in America

poll, a survey conducted by the National Sleep Foundation, people who were diagnosed with depression or anxiety were more likely to sleep less than six hours at night. The most common sleep disorder, insomnia, has the strongest link to depression. In a study of 10,000 people, those with insomnia were five times as likely to develop depression as those without it. In fact, insomnia is often one of the first symptoms of depression. Insomnia and depression feed on each other. Sleep loss often aggravates the symptoms of depression, and depression can make it more difficult to fall asleep. On the positive side, treating sleep problems can help depression and its symptoms, and vice versa.

5. **Negative effects on your skin.** Have you experienced puffy eyes after a few nights of missed sleep? Sleeplessness does affect your skin. It can lead to dull skin, fine lines, and dark circles under the eyes. When you don't get enough sleep, your body releases more of the stress hormone cortisol. In excess amounts, cortisol can break down skin collagen, the protein that keeps skin smooth and elastic. Sleep loss also causes the body to release too little human growth hormone. When we're young, human growth hormone promotes growth. As we age, it helps increase muscle mass, thicken skin, and strengthen bones.

7. **Loss of memory.** Do you want a sharp memory? Then get plenty of sleep. In 2009, American and French researchers determined that brain events called "sharp wave ripples" are responsible for consolidating memory. The ripples also transfer learned information from the hippocampus to the neocortex of the brain, where long-term memories are stored. Sharp wave ripples occur mostly during the deepest levels of sleep.

8. **Weight gain.** New studies indicate that losing sleep tends to make people eat more and gain weight. According to Matthew P. Walker (2013), an author of the study and a professor of psychology and neuroscience at the University of California, Berkeley, a sleepy brain appears to not only respond more strongly to junk food, but also has less ability to rein that impulse in. Not only does sleep loss appear to stimulate appetite,

but it also stimulates cravings for high-fat, high-carbohydrate foods. Ongoing studies are considering whether adequate sleep should be a standard part of weight-loss programs.

As you can see, sleep affects many areas of your life. It makes good health sense to get proper rest. Commit to going to bed at least thirty minutes earlier than you normally do. This seemingly small change in your lifestyle can make a huge difference in your overall health.

Benefits of Exercise

Statistics indicate that 60 percent of Americans don't get the recommended amount of physical activity. In fact, 25 percent of adults aren't active at all. We all have heard from the time that we were in elementary school about the health benefits gained from exercise—less stress, more confidence, better energy, and better memory. As adults, the benefits are even greater and more meaningful. Exercise controls your weight; boosts your energy level; promotes sleep; helps to fight diseases; and increases the sex drive. As amazing as those benefits are, it's not enough to get the majority of people in motion.

According to the *2008 Physical Activity Guidelines for Americans* put out by the U.S. Department of Health and Human Services, you need to do two types of physical activity—aerobics and muscle-strengthening—for at least 150 minutes each week to improve your health. So what will it really take to convince you to start a program at home for forty minutes a day for at least four times a week or twenty minutes a day every day?

As we focus on creating an amazing life, it again comes down to your making a decision to make positive changes in your life. You have to decide that you want to be healthy. To motivate yourself to exercise regularly, let's look at the psychological factors and think through the benefits.

1. **Exercise reverses the negative effects of stress.** Exercising for thirty minutes can blow off tension by increasing levels of "soothing" brain chemicals like serotonin, dopamine, and

norepinephrine. It can also work on a cellular level to reverse the stress toll on our aging process. A study conducted by the University of California found that stressed-out women who exercised vigorously for an average of forty-five minutes over a three-day period had cells that showed fewer signs of aging compared to women who were stressed and inactive.

2. **Exercise improves learning**. When you exercise, it increases the level of brain chemicals called growth factors. The growth factors help us to learn by making connections to our brain cells. Your brain cells are like muscles, you have to stretch them to get them to grow. Tennis and dance class are thought to give you the brain boost because you have to think about coordination.

3. **Exercise builds self-esteem and improves body image**. While this one is self-explanatory, the body changes don't have to be extreme to get a boost in your confidence. Small successes such as lifting ten pounds or more, running faster, or slimming down the waist one inch, can improve your self-esteem and body image.

4. **Exercise leaves you feeling euphoric**. There really is something called "runner's high." Doing exercises at high-intensity rate will set an exhilarated feeling all day.

5. **Exercise keeps the brain fit**. Mild activities, like a leisurely walk, can help keep your brain fit and active helping to combat memory loss and keeping vocabulary retrieval strong. It helps to maintain cognitive functioning particularly as you age. Studies have shown that activities such as cooking, gardening, and cleaning affect your cognition and memory positively. According to Harvard Medical School psychiatrist Dr. John Ratey, exercise is the single best thing you can do for your brain in terms of mood, memory, and learning. He proclaims that just ten minutes of activity changes your brain.

6. **Exercise may keep Alzheimer's at bay**. According to the Alzheimer's Research Center, exercise is one of the best weapons against the disease. Exercise appears to protect the

hippocampus, which governs memory and spatial navigation, and is one of the first brain regions to succumb to Alzheimer's-related damage.

So, did that give you some additional reasons to get into gear and set a schedule for some type of regular exercise? Remember, it starts with a decision on your part.

Yoga and Meditation

There are many different types of exercise; it's a matter of trying out different activities to find the one that works for you and that you find enjoyable so you'll be encouraged to stick with it. I recommend one particular form of exercise, which is widely known for focusing on mind, body, *and* spirit: yoga. This activity originated in India and has been practiced for about 5,000 years. It's estimated that eleven million Americans are now enjoying the benefits of yoga. These benefits include alleviating health problems, reducing stress, and making the spine supple. I have attended yoga classes, and can attest to the benefits of focusing on breathing, clearing your mind, being tuned in with your body, and having proper posture.

A study headed by Chris Streeter, MD, and colleagues at Boston University conducted with the Division of Psychiatry at Boston University School of Medicine, found that three sessions of yoga per week boosted participants' levels of the brain chemical GABA, which typically translates into improved mood and decreased anxiety helping to ward off depression. Though it doesn't substitute for drug treatment for depression, the study's researchers said yoga can be used to complement the medication. Yoga focuses on breathing, one of the lifelines to our well-being. Learning breathing techniques through yoga and meditation can provide benefits to your overall health. Breathing drives the nervous system and provides 99 percent of your energy. Without energy, nothing works. So breathe deep!

Hopefully, the information in this chapter has convinced you that you have full control over your health and fitness. So, what's stopping you from being as healthy as you can be?

Roadmap

1. **Internalize that you are in control of your health**. Repeat the phrase, "I am in the driver's seat and I am in control of my health." This will continue to help you change any negative thought patterns you may have about your body.

2. **Commit to adopting a healthy lifestyle**. Lifestyle is all about the choices that you make every day. In order to become healthy you have to change your current habits and replace them with new habits. For example, incorporating a new habit such as regular exercise and extra sleep into your life requires you to take a look at your daily schedule and see what can either be deleted or better managed to make room for these new healthy lifestyle choices.

3. **Avoid criticizing yourself and negative talk**. When your body doesn't look like you want it to, it's easy to fall into negative self-talk, such as, "I can't believe I let myself get out of shape," or "You should be ashamed. You look like a pig." Instead, change your words to project positive images of yourself. For example, "I would like to be healthy and I am working to get there. I know that there are things that I can do better, and I am doing it."

4. **Avoid focusing on a particular size**. Don't get caught up in thinking that the success of your weight has to do with fitting into a particular size. Everyone is not built to be a size two or four. Your plan should focus on your health and not your size.

5. **Reward yourself**. Another key to motivation is to reward yourself when you have accomplished a goal. Avoid using food as your main reward. It is okay to reward yourself with a piece of

chocolate cake every once in a while, but find other rewards that you can treat yourself to more often that will make you feel accomplished.

6. **If you fall off the wagon, just get back on**. You will have times that you slip and eat something or a day when exercise is skipped. Don't get discouraged—and don't make excuses to turn one off day into a series of off days. Forgive yourself, get back on track, and keep it moving.

ELEVEN

A Firm Grip on Your Wallet

Taming Your Finances

H OW MANY TIMES have you bought something or went somewhere you couldn't afford? There was a nagging thought in the back (or front) of your mind that you tried to silence. You questioned yourself and even looked at your bank account, but you decided to go ahead and make the purchase or take the trip anyway. You rationalized it in your mind because you wanted to enjoy the benefits of an object or experience. Maybe it was clothing, shoes, appliances, technology, cars, etc. Or, maybe you wanted to go on an outing or take a trip, but you had limited resources. While you were there, you forced yourself to have a good time, but you couldn't get rid of the gnawing feeling that you were somewhere you really shouldn't have been, and, to top it off, you have to limit your good time because of what was *not* in your wallet. In case you are unclear on what I mean by "can't afford," I have listed some clues for you.

You know that you can't afford "the trip" when:

- You haven't paid all of the bills that are due.
- You have to pay for the trip with credit cards.
- You haven't planned ahead and saved for the trip.
- You have to borrow money to go.

Show Me the Money

Money is one of the most important factors in determining the quality of your journey in life, so it's critical to have your finances in order. Money can be an emotionally charged subject. As mentioned in the previous chapter, money, or the lack thereof, is one of the factors that cause stress and depression. During recessions and other difficult economic times, the number of those suffering from depression, and the rate of suicide, increase. In fact, according to the Centers for Disease Control, 13.4 percent of individuals who committed suicide during the United States' 2007 to 2009 recession had experienced job and financial difficulties.

Often when you hear or see the word "money" you experience an immediate reaction. Is the feeling positive or negative? Do you feel excited, afraid, hopeful, motivated, sad, or depressed? The answer to this question could hold the key to where you are right now financially. In this chapter, we will address the importance of the thoughts driving your actions and decisions, which then affect your bank account. The goal is to help you change your attitude, thoughts, words, and energy about money by helping you to understand the psychological barriers that have blocked you. Throughout this chapter you will be given tips and advice on how to make decisions about your finances that will help you create a plan to achieve your financial goals. We will start with looking at some things that can hinder the flow of your finances—your thoughts, values, spending habits, lifestyle choices, and general money knowledge, among them.

What Do You Believe about Money?

According to a report by the Boston Consulting Group (BCG), global wealth hit a record $121.8 trillion high in 2010 or $20 trillion above pre-recession levels. In addition, the number of millionaire households jumped 12.2 percent to about 12.5 million. The BCG predicts that this trend will continue up to about $162 trillion by 2015, "driven by the performance of the capital markets and the growth of GDP in countries around the world." The report also notes that "wealth will grow fastest in emerging markets." So where are the millionaires? There are plenty throughout the world, with the United States having its fair share. According to the BCG, 5.2 million U.S. households have more than a million dollars in assets compared to $1.5 million in Japan and $1.1 million in China.

The question is, if wealth abounds—$5.2 trillion in just 5.2 million U.S. households, and much more money in the country if you account for the assets of the entire U.S. population—why are so few people rich? Can't it be distributed differently?

I have heard some people say that there's only a small cohort of privileged people who are able to access great wealth. If you believe that only a limited number of people are meant to be wealthy, then you are keeping yourself from financial success.

There is a distinct difference between thoughts of scarcity and thoughts of abundance. In my experience, I have found that many non-native Americans think in terms of abundance. I have seen countless interviews on news programs with immigrants who come to America with so many strikes against them and they still succeed. One particular interview from the show *Undercover Boss* featured a man who had recently emigrated from Pakistan and was working as a delivery truck driver on the night shift. His job wasn't ideal, yet he was cheerful, helpful, and dedicated, and everyone liked him. His attitude was extremely positive. When asked about his job and why he seemed so happy, despite working the midnight shift for mediocre wages, he explained that he had come to this country several years ago with his family and only fifty dollars in his pocket. He didn't know anyone or the language, but he has since been able to build a life for himself and his family. Toward the end of the interview, he began to tear up. He said, "You here in America just don't understand the opportunity. You are here and take it for granted because you don't understand how great it is, coming from another country and being able to make it."

I believe that says it all. It is easy to have the abundance mentality when you come from scarcity, but it's damaging when you come from a country of abundance, free enterprise, and opportunity, yet embrace the scarcity mindset that there is little opportunity here.

Are your beliefs about money affecting the direction of your cash flow? Before we continue, let's stop and take a look at some of your beliefs.

REST STOP

It is important to evaluate your money–belief system. Your ideas about money hold the key to your money success, because what you think and believe will determine your actions. In your notebook, write the numbers one through ten. Answer yes or no beside each number that coincides with the question.

Money Values Test		
1. Do you believe that money is the root of all evil?	Yes	No
2. Do you believe that money tends to corrupt people?	Yes	No
3. Do you believe that you don't deserve to be rich?	Yes	No
4. Do you believe that there is virtue in having less?	Yes	No
5. Do you believe more money equates to more problems?	Yes	No
6. Do you believe that you will never be a millionaire?	Yes	No
7. Do you believe that rich people are seldom happy?	Yes	No
8. Do you believe you need a lot of money to make money?	Yes	No
9. Do you believe you need to work more jobs to make more money?	Yes	No
10. Do you believe you will always be in debt?	Yes	No

If you answered yes to five or more of the questions, your major belief is that money is negative and it would have a negative impact in your life. If you have three to four yeses, you are struggling with the concept of money being a positive factor in your life and there is some fear that holds you back from the desire to seek more wealth. If you answered one to two yeses, you have a slight hesitation that could inhibit money from flowing freely.

--- --- --- --- --- --- --- --- --- --- --- --- --- --- --- --- --- --- --- ---

Scarcity or Abundance Test

In what direction do you lean when it comes to money? Do you consider there to be an insufficient supply, a shortage, or do you think it is more than plentiful? To see which side of the table you are on, look at the statements below. In your notebook, write the numbers one through nine. Read the statements under each column. Write down the word from the column that you agree with (example: 1. scarcity 2. abundance). Be honest in your thoughts.

Scarcity	Abundance
1. The amount of money I can make is limited.	1. The amount of money I can make is unlimited.
2. Great opportunities only exist for a few people.	2. Great opportunities exist for everyone.
3. Money is reserved for the rich and famous.	3. I can create my own money source.
4. There is a glass ceiling.	4. Money is for everyone.
5. Money does not grow on trees.	5. Money actually does come from trees, and I want my own tree.
6. We are in competition with each other. May the best person win.	6. Although others may do what I do, there is plenty of opportunity for us all.
7. There are only a few winners.	7. Everyone can be a winner at something.
8. Immigrants have better opportunities than I do.	8. We have the same opportunities as immigrants.
9. It's better to save all my money. I never know when the rainy day will come.	9. What is for me is for me. If I didn't get the job, opportunity, or deal, I wasn't supposed to.

Which side of the table did you mostly agree with?

Your Money Language

Just as your words matter when it comes to every other area of your life, they are also critical when it comes to money. Your "money language" is vitally important to your financial success. Think about what you say about money on a daily basis. Have you said any of the following?

- I am broke.
- I can't afford that.
- The government takes all my money.
- I don't make enough money for that.
- It's hard to make it.
- Money is not my friend.
- It's the recession.
- I don't have any money right now.
- Rich people have all the money.
- I don't need more money; it will bring more problems.
- Money is trouble.
- Money doesn't buy you happiness.
- I'm too old to start chasing dreams.

This list could go on and on. Have you spoken these words or heard someone else verbalize the sentences? Remember, you speak your reality.

Your Money Energy

Your physical, mental, emotional, and spiritual energies all react and respond to money. You either attract it to you or repel it with the barriers, consciously and/or subconsciously, that you have in place.

When money flows to you, do you in turn move it forward to someone else? Alternatively, do you keep it all for yourself and wait for more to come? When you keep money flowing to others, it will come back to you in greater measures. This is biblically explained as the "reap and sow" principle. Examples of moving money forward are giving to charities, helping others in need, or performing random acts of kindness. In order to get money and have it flow to you, you have to be willing for it to flow *through* you. You may wonder why some people continue to get wealthy. Many times, it is that they have mastered the success of money principles, money knowledge, and the mindset that is required in order to continue to create money flow.

Your Money Relationship

We have tested your money beliefs and talked about your money energy, but what is your actual *relationship* with money—meaning how does it affect your behavior and feelings?

I need to challenge you to think very concretely right now about relationships. In a romantic relationship, the goals for you and your partner are to be in love, increase the depth and intensity of your relationship, experience peace, have fun, enjoy each other, build dreams, and respect and value each other. These goals are accomplished when you put forth the effort to make them happen. You have to work together, make plans, spend time together, learn each other's needs and wants, love one another through the difficulties, and treat each other with respect.

Think about those goals in terms of money and what you would like for it to do for you. Your goals are to increase its flow, have fun, build your dreams, bring value to your life, and experience peace. These things will happen as you learn to connect with your money. You can't be afraid of it— or avoid, ignore, or disrespect it—and hope that it will bring you peace. Just like a relationship with another person, your financial goals will only happen when you spend time with your money, make plans for it, understand how it works, and value it through the good times and the bad times.

Getting Through a Financial Crisis

In Chapter 1, I talked about being lost. Millions of people have found themselves lost after experiencing an unfortunate life event, such as a job layoff, factory plant closing, divorce, natural disaster, or a relative's or friend's death; all can immediately and profoundly affect your financial status. As I mentioned previously, my life changed when I went through a divorce. Divorce is generally not something that you prepare for. You don't get married and then work and save money to someday live a separate life. So, most people naturally are not prepared for divorce when it happens and haven't thought about what it will look like for them.

The fact that I was working as an entrepreneur made the financial impact of my divorce even more devastating. Moreover, it happened during the 2008 to 2009 financial instability that the United States experienced. During that time I, like all business owners, slept lightly and was afraid to exhale, hoping that my company could weather the economic storm. I had been meeting with four different companies with proposals for training their employees in the area of emotional health and wellness. The proposals for the four companies altogether came to a cost of almost $150,000 worth of services. In any type of sales capacity, you know that occasionally the "sales process" can take some time. I had been meeting with these companies over several months. All systems were a go—or so I thought. Things took a sudden turn for the worse when, for one reason or another, each company had to back out of their commitment. All of the revenue I had anticipated disappeared within two months. Then within a month of that financial fiasco, my husband moved out. While I knew the move was coming, it was horrible timing to assume fifteen extra bills in the process. Talk about life changing dramatically in a short period. *Help me!* I thought, *Now what do I do?*

Your story may look different. It may be that you lost your job or your house or you faced some other financial adversity. Whatever the case may be, it can be devastating to you and affect you mentally, physically, and spiritually. There are some specific steps to help you regain emotional stability.

ROAD TO RECOVERY IN FINANCIAL CRISIS

1. **Allow yourself to feel**. You are going to have emotions of all kinds. You may feel shock, denial, betrayal, anger, hurt, confusion, embarrassment, etc. Whatever you are feeling, by all means, let it out. Releasing your emotions will help you through the healing process quicker. When you can acknowledge your emotions, you are on your way to understanding how to manage them.

2. **Give yourself a time limit to grieve**. This is important so that you don't get caught up in wallowing in your sorrow. I gave myself three days to lie around feeling sad, cry, and be upset. After that, I had to make a conscious decision to refocus my energy on solutions.

3. **Reprogram your thinking**. It's easy for your mind to fixate on the unfortunate aspects of the situation. Your mind will be bombarded with all types of thoughts, most of which will be negative. You will second-guess yourself and your instincts, your confidence, and your intellect. Just know that is part of the normal process. Eventually, you must block the negative thoughts and replace them with something positive. Self-talk is required.

4. **Find the lessons learned**. Get out your notebook and begin to think about lessons learned from the experience. Writing down lessons forces you to start thinking about the good that the situation is bringing to you and helps you to own your part of the responsibility in the outcome.

5. **Create a plan focusing on solutions**. Your plan has to focus on solving your immediate problems. You are shifting your mind into the logical thinking space so that it will not be hampered by your emotions, and you will be able to analytically process information and create solutions.

6. **Look for opportunities**. This is where you can enlist the help of others. Let people know that you are looking for specific opportunities. Don't be afraid to disclose your current situation, for example, "I was downsized," "I'm going through a divorce," etc. Have an open mind when looking for new opportunities. They are everywhere.

7. **Continue to develop your mind, body, and spirit**. Nourish your mind and spirit with self-talk, positive thinking, inspirational literature, prayer, meditation, and music. Develop your body by sticking with and beefing up your exercise routine. Revisit Chapter 10 to see the benefits of exercising for your brain.

Money and Your Lifestyle Choices

At this time, we will examine how your perspective on a financial crisis can influence your choices and decisions. Just like lemons don't turn to lemonade on their own, you turning the bad into good is a choice. To illustrate this, let's look at two men faced with the same bad thing happening to them.

Jim had worked at the factory plant in his city for twenty-six years. He had been with the company since its inception and had weathered many of the economic storms the company faced throughout the years. He had built a comfortable life for his family and was planning to retire in ten years at the age of sixty. Suddenly one day, news spread like wildfire that the plant was closing for good in three months. Jim was devastated. What was he going to do? He wasn't financially ready for retirement, because it wasn't supposed to happen for another ten years. He was fifty; who would hire someone at that age, especially when all his experience was in factory work? He had no other job skills and felt like his life was ending.

Calvin worked for the same plant for twenty years. He also had been through difficulties with his company. The life he built for his family was nice, but they lived on a tight budget to maintain it. While he had also planned to retire one day, it wasn't with this company. He had a vision to one day start his own flower shop. On the weekends, he spent much of his time in his garden, which was full of many beautiful flowers that he planted so that he could understand everything about them. When he heard the news of the factory's shutdown, he knew in his heart that this was his opportunity to make his dream come true. He had planned to work at the plant for two more years, so he hadn't quite saved all the money he needed to open his shop, but that was okay. He knew that he would have to plan around it and make it work. He felt like his life was just beginning.

In your notebook, write out all of the differences that you can find between Jim and Calvin. Look at their actions, plans, and thoughts. They found themselves in the same circumstances with their jobs, yet they had different outcomes. Calvin's outlook was different because he had a plan B that helped him to get through his difficulty. As you think about these stories, apply them to your life. What has happened that you can look at as an opportunity instead of the end of the road? Do you have a plan B and maybe a plan C? If you want to stay at your current job (or in your current marriage), it's important to think about what you would do if financial tragedy should occur. And this would include a spouse dying, not just divorcing you.

It's critical to be prepared for whatever life may bring.

Creating Financial Success

You have tested your beliefs and you've looked at some of your thought patterns to help you understand your money perspective. Now it's time to think about an upward trajectory in terms of your money. What better way to learn than to look at those who have fat wallets?

Who Wants to Be a Millionaire?

I have spent a great deal of money and time researching, learning, and studying millionaires to understand how they live and think and what their daily habits are. What makes them unique? Most of the multimillionaires that I know are all self-made, which means that they carved out their own destiny in some way. Yet recall from the beginning of this chapter: If money exists and is available for everyone, why are so few people experiencing wealth? It's not because there is this small segment of the population that has been singled out to succeed. It has to do with the mindset of those who are wealthy and their thoughts, habits, and way of living, which is different from the lifestyle of the vast majority of people.

Just how different is the mindset? Steve Siebold, who interviewed hundreds of wealthy people over a twenty-seven-year period, and presented his findings in his book *How Rich People Think*. He noted that rich people have certain psychological behavior patterns that differ from those who aren't rich. Here is a comparison chart I've created based on Siebold's book that lists a few of the mental thought patterns of the rich vs. those who are middle class or poor.

Middle Class/Poor Money Ideas	Rich Money Ideas
Spend It — When I have money, I spend it. I never know when I will get more.	*Invest It* — Money is about how to invest what I have in order to make more.
Emotional — Pursue money based on how it makes me feel, both positively and negatively.	*Logical* — Pursue money using the logical portions of the brain; there are principles that are applied in order to make money.
Thoughts — Think small and limit about the amount of money that I can make.	*Thoughts* — Feel like there is no limit to the amount of money that can be made.
Goals — Little or no money defined goals. Just flow with life and how it happens.	*Goals* — Money goals are set and defined to create a structured way of living.

Worries — About money and the lack thereof.	**Dreams** — About money and its abundance.
Children — Teach them to survive.	**Children** — Teach them how to be rich.
Entertainment — Live for and thrive on being entertained; enjoy TV, radio, playing/watching games, and hanging out.	**Education** — Live and thrive on learning new ideas, information, and investing in materials/information that will help me achieve my goals.
Linear reason for work — Work to retire.	**Global reason to work** — Work to make an impact on the world.
Perspective — Wait for the ship to come in.	**Perspective** — Build the ship.
View of Economy — Recession.	**View of Economy** — Opportunity.
Single stream of income — Salaried jobs and hourly wages are the way to make money.	**Multiple streams of income** — Believe that income comes through several facets, multilevel marketing, ideas, investments, etc.

Those are just a few of the differences in the mental thought patterns that govern the lives of the rich and the poor. Did you see yourself and your thought patterns in the chart? It is easy to see how opposing these thoughts are when they are side by side. Your thoughts and beliefs about money stem from your upbringing, values, and experiences. You received the programming from childhood, which informs your thoughts and beliefs in adulthood. The great news is that you can always change your thinking, so let's work to change your mind.

Steps to Transform Your Mind for Financial Success

In this section, I will focus on the steps you need to take to get your life in a place of abundance. As with everything else worth achieving, it is going to take commitment, work, and dedication. If your finances are not where you would like them to be, it did not happen overnight and it will not be fixed overnight. Keep your notebook handy because there will be questions that you will need to think about and answer in each section. We have already discussed a great deal about thoughts and words, so the following points will be action-oriented strategies.

1. Take full responsibility for where you are right now.

No more blame game. I know that situations and events do contribute to where you may find yourself, but you don't have to be stagnant. You have to be able to admit that you are responsible for being where you are. Even if your situation has come with some circumstances that are beyond your control, you can still recover and come out on top.

In your notebook, write down what responsibility you have for your current situation. What could you have done differently? What can you do now to change your current situation?

2. Be a good manager of your current budget and more will come.

This tip is similar to the biblical scripture, "You were faithful with a few things, and I will put you in charge of many things." Think about it. Isn't that how it pretty much works in life? With any job, you start out at the bottom of the ladder. The more you prove you can handle the responsibilities given to you, the more you can move up and handle greater tasks. It's the same with managing your finances.

The first question is, do you have a budget? Research estimates that only about 40 percent of households follow a budget. When all financial experts say that budgeting is one of the key strategies for being in control of your money, why are you not practicing it? The famous axiom, "If you fail to plan, you plan to fail" is true here. A budget is your plan for your money. If you are not doing an effective job at managing a

$50,000 annual salary, what makes you think you can handle $100,000 salary? If you are "broke" now, you will be just as broke or worse with more money because you are living with the mentality of spending instead of investing.

The second question is if you have a budget, are you adhering to it? In order to stick to a budget, you need to know where your money is going. This means that if you don't already, you'll need to start keeping track of your expenditures.

In your notebook, write the answers to these questions: Do you have a budget? Why or why not? If you do, are you using it effectively to stay in control of your money?

If you need to download a simple budget plan, go to www.creating amazinglives.com and click on the money tab.

3. Create cash flow with your current income.

Cash flow is the pattern of income and expenses and its consequences for how much money is available at a given time. You may think that having cash flow is impossible, since you feel as if you don't have enough money already. It's not impossible. It requires taking inventory of your current expenses and decreasing or cutting out unnecessary expenses. It may be that you need to be creative and look for ways to combine things. For example, once while I was figuring out my expenses, I called the phone company to see if there was a way to modify my services. I was paying for a second phone line and found I could save $40 a month if I bundled that line with my other services. That is a savings of $480 a year. An extra $15, $20, or $25 per month really adds up.

What is in your expenses that you really don't need or use? What unnecessary services do you have that you can eliminate? Find the small things and work your way up to the larger items. Are you renting furniture or other items? How many times are you eating out, going for drinks, or buying things you want but don't need? I challenge you to save an extra $150 to $200 each month by decreasing your spending. (This is where a budget comes in handy, because if you aren't recording how much you're spending and where you're spending it, it's harder to know where to cut back.)

4. Strive to live within your means.

There are millions of people who are living far beyond their cash flow. The trend of the century has become *dress to impress, drive to impress,* and *live to impress.* My question is, who are you trying to impress and why do you care about them? So many people who complain that they are broke have designer shoes, bags, and purses and are driving luxury vehicles. Having these impressive items somehow seems to fill a need they have to look and feel important. If you can afford to wear, carry, or drive labels, I am the first one to celebrate you, but if you can't afford these things—meaning you can't pay cash for the items—what is the real value and benefit of having them? They are contributing to you being broke, and worse, in debt, and what's impressive about that?

According to the New York Federal Quarterly Report, as of March 2013, Americans have $11.23 trillion dollars of credit card debt. How much of that percentage belongs to you? Avoiding credit card debt is vital to your financial stability.

In your notebook, answer the following questions.

    a) Are you living in a home you can afford?

    b) Are you driving a car you can afford?

    c) Do you spend money on clothes that you can't afford?

    d) Who are you trying to impress?

5. *Learn to give to receive.*

This principle isn't just about giving money or tangible items; it's about giving your time and energy. Early on I learned the principle of giving and have passed the legacy to my children. Twice a year, we will clean out our closets and donate clothing to charitable organizations and shelters. I have given away furniture, a car, and other tangible items. Being able to give to others is one of the greatest feelings, so it becomes a gift to you as well. Remember, if your hands are closed so tightly around your stuff, they will never be open to receive.

Take inventory of your stuff. In your notebook, make a list of what is in your closet, home, garage, or storage that you can give to someone else who may be in need. Write down a list of charities/organizations that you donate your things to. Think of the last time that you gave something away to someone. Write how that made you feel. Duplicate that feeling as often as you can.

6. Use the three-rule principle.

Have you ever tried to live on 70 percent of your net earnings? The three-rule principle has you doing just that, and for many people that I have studied and read about, the principle works. Where does the other 30 percent go? Here are the principles:

a)   Pay yourself 10 percent of your earnings.
b)   Give a church or charity 10 percent of your earnings.
c)   Save or invest 10 percent of your earnings.

That leaves 70 percent of your earnings to pay your expenses. It's important to pay yourself so that you don't feel neglected or that you work hard and can't even treat yourself. When you give to a charity or a church, you are continuing the money flow and the reciprocity principle. Saving and investing a set portion each month will help you to reach your goals for ensuring that you have an emergency fund.

Maybe you have heard this all before and have even tried to use this principle but felt like it didn't work. I challenge you to commit to it for at least three months and see what happens. Will you try it?

In your notebook, make a commitment that you will try the 70 percent rule for at least three months and keep track of how it makes you feel.

7. Create Additional Streams of Income through Direct Marketing and Sales

This tip is about opening your mind to see all of the money-making opportunities around you. I attended classes a few years ago that taught the concept of multiple streams of income and direct/network marketing was one of the top ways to create additional revenue. I was happy to have a jump start on understanding other streams of income because I had started selling Amway products at the ripe age of fourteen. I've always been attracted to direct marketing companies as a way to earn extra money, and I've made thousands of dollars in the process. What has always surprised me is that when talking to people about direct marketing companies, several "broke" people thought they were too good to be involved in "one of those" companies. I was very intrigued by the mindset of so many people who could see others making money yet say or think to themselves, *That's not for me.* The barriers that block you from exploring other ways to increase cash flow will only keep you in a broke state. After approaching individuals with the idea of exploring the opportunity of joining a direct marketing company, I would hear things like, "That sounds like a get-rich-quick scheme." Now to that comment I ask, "Who wants to get rich slowly?" Many people are under the impression that you can sign up with a company as an independent distributor, but you don't have to work at it. Moreover, because there is no strategic effort put in to make it work, they walk away saying, "It doesn't work." There again is the mentality that I talked about earlier, the expectation of getting something for nothing. I have no idea how so many people have fallen into the space of wanting things without doing the work. That is not reality. Again, we reap what we sow, or put another way, we get out of something what we put into it.

Now I will be the first to say that there are certain skills needed in order to be successful at generating additional income through direct marketing, just as certain skills are needed with any business. There are three companies I would recommend if you are contemplating making money in the direct marketing industry. I have worked with each of these companies and can vouch for their infrastructure, leadership, and success, as well as the quality of their products.

MARY KAY

There is probably not a person around who hasn't heard of Mary Kay cosmetics. This Dallas-based privately owned company sells cosmetic products directly to consumers using multilevel marketing. According to the 2013 edition of *Direct Selling News*, Mary Kay was the sixth largest direct-selling company in the world in 2013, with net sales of $3.1 billion. Mary Kay Ash's founding principles—God first, family second, and career third—has helped the company to grow to productive levels and has even enabled some women to become millionaires.

TRACI LYNN FASHION JEWELRY

Traci Lynn Fashion Jewelry was established in 1989 in Philadelphia by its founder and president, Dr. Traci Lynn. For nearly twenty years, Traci Lynn Fashion Jewelry has sold high-quality, affordable fashion jewelry through a wholesale network and direct sales. Through this national company, products are delivered through consultants to customers via home or office shows, personal shopping, and catalog orders.

MELALEUCA

Melaleuca is a wellness company that sells nutritional supplements, cleaning supplies, and personal-care products, which are distributed through direct sales through independent reps internationally. Many of its products are made with the melaleuca plant and do not contain harmful toxins or chemicals. They offer safe and effective cleaning products for households and businesses. The company has also surpassed a billion dollars in sales.

I have worked at one time or another as a distributor or as a coach for each of these companies and can recommend their products, leadership, and potential for cash flow (for more information on any of these companies, please visit www.creatingamazinglives.com). But these are just three of hundreds of companies that exist in national, regional, or local markets that you can sign on with as an independent contractor to create additional monies in whatever amount of time you decide to designate for it.

In addition to direct-selling companies, there are other industries that can help you create supplemental income. Here are a handful of ideas:

- Online businesses
- Freelance writing
- Freelance photography
- Personal training
- Dog walking
- Tutoring
- Bookkeeping

REST STOP

If you've been using credit cards to "make" your budget or you don't know how you can live by the 70 percent principle when you need 100 percent to pay all your bills, earning extra income can help you get out of debt and having your priorities in order with your finances. If that is your case, in your notebook, write your plan on what you will do to increase your cash flow and opportunities. Include in the plan how you will shift your thinking about money that will allow it to flow to you. As American author and motivational speaker Zig Ziglar, said, "Money isn't the most important thing in life, but it's reasonably close to oxygen on the 'gotta have it' scale."

Roadmap

1. **You are in the driver's seat when it comes to your finances**. The first step to taking control is understanding that you have power over your finances. Believe that. Next, act on that belief. As in every area of your life, you make the decisions about your money. So decide where you would like your money to go and plan accordingly.

2. **Work every day to change your thoughts**. Your thoughts and beliefs about money are deeply rooted and take time to change. It will require major effort and a plan that includes daily affirmations and reading materials and information to help flush out negativity that may surround your thinking.

3. **Look at the people in your circle**. The saying "Birds of a feather flock together" carries weight. More than likely the friends in your social circle have the same thoughts and perceptions about money that you do. Invest in getting to know people who have an abundance mindset.

4. **Invest in yourself**. Set aside money to invest in learning, programs, and self-development. It is critical to keep your mind open to learning. There are tons of programs that are available that will help you to learn new information, industries, and opportunities.

5. **Stop wasting your valuable time**. Examine where and how you are spending your time. You will be surprised to find that you are wasting time watching TV, talking on the phone, or browsing the Internet instead of using the time to create opportunities for yourself. I challenge you to turn off your TV, phone, and computer and start letting your creative juices flow—you might think of something that will enhance your income.

6. **Explore at least one additional stream of income**. Challenge yourself to take advantage of the many companies and opportunities that exist in the land of plenty. Remember there is money out there and it circulates to those who want it, so go get it.

TWELVE

The Bridges, Tunnels, and Mountain Passes of Life

Finding Joy and Peace Through Spirituality

T HE TRIP HOME to see her parents took nine hours by car. Maggie had driven home many times before and knew that if she timed it just right she could make it there before dark. She didn't get to leave as early as she planned and calculated that she was running about two hours behind. *I will just drive a little faster,* she thought, to make up for lost time. The ride was smooth until she noticed a few raindrops on the window shield. The sun seemed to go down quickly as the raindrops picked up their pace. Within fifteen minutes, the sun had completely disappeared and the rain was increasing. Maggie began to slow her pace. Not only was she not fond of driving at night, but she also dreaded the rain. As she began to adjust the windshield wipers, she noticed the truck in front of her was swerving. She tapped her brakes to slow down, but her tires couldn't find their traction on the wet ground. Her car began to slide and spin just as the car behind her slid as well and caught her left rear bumper. In a split second, she heard a deafening crash and that was all she remembered. Although Maggie survived the crash, the intermittent pains in her back and knee are constant reminders about how her life had changed in an instant.

You probably have experienced some type of an "accident" on your journey thus far, when an event stopped you in your tracks and changed the course or direction of your life. It may have been sickness, an accident, the loss of a loved one, an addiction, or a devastation of some other kind. The many twists, turns, ups, downs, detours, roadblocks, collisions, and unforeseen events can fill your life with turmoil. We always want joy in our lives and seek for peace and serenity but we especially long for it during challenging times.

Profound emotions such as peace and serenity can only be found deep within your soul and require a spiritual connection. In this chapter, I will be discussing the significance of a healthy spirit. Keep in mind that the focus is on spirituality, not religion. While religion has its place in our society, I believe spirituality is the personal part that only has to do with you and your relationship with God or another higher power. I will also give suggestions and tips on how to connect your spirit to God and how that translates to living an amazing life on this journey, in spite of any difficult circumstances or challenges that may arise.

When Tragedy Strikes

Everyone's spirit and faith are tested at one point or another. I can speak from personal experience of a very harrowing time in my life. After some challenges with infertility, I became pregnant with triplets. Elation turned to sorrow when I lost one of the babies, but I was still very excited to welcome my twins into the world. I thought life could not be more perfect.

As you can imagine, there was a great deal of preparation and shopping! I had to purchase double of everything a new parent would need: cribs, car seats, clothes, diapers, and high chairs. Amid all of the excitement, I went into premature labor at twenty-six weeks.

Doctors tried everything possible to stop the contractions, but after a week of drugs and heavy sedation, the babies were ready to come into the world and no one could stop them. I had a son, Charles, who was two pounds and two ounces, and a daughter, Chelsie, one pound and nine ounces. The fragility of a tiny life was magnified beyond measure as I saw my babies fit into the palm of the doctor's hands.

Things moved at a rapid pace as the doctor came in and informed us that our daughter had a heart defect called Tetralogy of Fallot (*teh-tral-uh-je ov fuh-LOE*), a rare heart condition combining four heart defects that are present at birth. These defects, which affect the structure of the heart, cause oxygen-poor blood to flow out of the heart and into the rest of the body. We were informed there was a 70 percent chance that she would *not* survive. Immediately, I begin to pray and hold onto my faith.

The next day, just as I began to settle in my mind that we would be watching our babies grow at the hospital, I heard a "code blue" over the intercom. My heart stopped as the phone rang and the nurse said, "We need you in the NICU. Something has happened to one of your babies." When they wheeled me in, I saw a group of staff surrounding my son. They were trying to resuscitate him. He had gone into cardiac arrest. The doctor and the nurses worked to resuscitate him, but he was already gone. My thoughts swirled in my head as I felt sick and my body and mind were wracked with pain. I thought, *What just happened? That was my healthy child!* That night they brought him to me to hold. I held his lifeless, tiny, cold body in my arms and prayed that I could give him *my* breath.

At twenty-seven years old, I was planning my child's funeral. Planning a funeral for your child is never something that fits into your psyche. It defies the normal cycle of life. The sun was shining bright as I looked through the window of the black limo riding to the cemetery. It looked like every other normal day, but it wasn't. I could barely walk to where we had his services and was laid to rest. My mind, body, and spirit were all in turmoil, and peace was nowhere to be found.

The next few days were filled with agony, pain, anxiety, shock—and gratitude that I had one baby left. Chelsie was extremely sick and very tiny, but I knew that she could make it. She was highly sensitive and could not be held much. She was too small for an operation and she wasn't getting enough oxygen into her system to grow. Then, when

Chelsie was a month old, I discovered that the doctors had caused Charles's death. They had inserted his umbilical catheter too far and it made a loop into his heart, causing the cardiac arrest.

The pain now turned into anger and confusion. I thought, *Why hadn't they told us?* These same doctors who were caring for my precious daughter had accidentally killed my son. The agony I felt was indescribable. Chelsie was too sick to move to another hospital, but how could I trust them? As time moved on, I was filled with anxiety. On Thanksgiving, Chelsie's heart stopped and we almost lost her. Once again, her fighting spirit pulled her through. Each day she became more alert, but wasn't growing. The celebration of the New Year came and went. I was praying for the faith that would heal my daughter's heart. The second week into the new year, the doctors came and said they were doing all they could but she was not getting better. They wanted me and my husband to decide if we should take her off life support. I thought, *What? No, No, She is alive, alert, and can smile, and you want be to take away her ability to breathe?*

It was the twenty-second day of January when Chelsie crashed again. Doctors were able to restart her heart and continued to pump medicine into her little body. Her heart beat for a minute on its own and then it stopped again.

"Try just one more time," I begged and cried. They pumped more medicine into her tiny body and then everything shut down. She just couldn't go one more beat. I started out with three babies and ended up with none. I felt incredibly lost and helpless. After all, nobody teaches someone how to be a "used to be" mother.

There was yet another casket and *another* funeral. Chelsie's funeral was large with people coming from out of state to say goodbye to my little angel. She had touched so many of our family and friends in the three-and-a-half months that she was here. There were so many people who had prayed for her.

As for me, I thought, *How can I ever smile again? How could God do this to me?* My spirit and faith were shattered. I had prayed for the healing of my children, and instead they were taken from me. The next year was incredibly dark. I went into a deep depression. I didn't know that it was possible to feel so much pain, nor did I realize that your body could get to a point that it couldn't produce any more tears. I even wanted my life to end since the pain seemed unbearable.

I realized that even though you are living, you can die mentally, emotionally, and spiritually. But, with the help of counselors and support groups, I was able to keep going. We filed a lawsuit against the doctors who accidentally killed my son. Although we had all the evidence to prove their guilt, a weeklong court trial resulted in a not-guilty verdict rendered by the jury. I couldn't believe it. How could they not be guilty when they admitted killing my son? This wasn't an episode of *LA Law*. It was real. I was filled with intense anger, and my feelings of confusion, unforgiveness, and injustice wreaked havoc on my body and spirit.

I had to go through the journey of reinventing my faith, my beliefs, and myself. That was not an easy task. To cope with the devastation, I sought help from clergy, counselors, and support groups. I was at the beauty parlor one day when things began to change. I met a lady there who could sense the deep sadness in my spirit and invited me to visit her church. She was the wife of the church's pastor and said that she had been praying for me. Because she didn't know me, or my story, I knew that God had placed her in my life to help guide me. She became a significant part of rebuilding my faith. I could now understand the significance of a spiritual connection. It was not about having an easier life than those who don't have spirituality; it was about having God to lean on during the difficult times. Even though you don't have all the answers, your heart can be at peace knowing that you are not alone. I realized the true meaning of faith is total *trust* in God no matter what happens.

What helps during the tough time of an "accident" on the course of your journey in life is having faith in God and believing that God, the Creator, loves and cares for you, his creation. It is important to believe that he is there with you in your darkest hour even though you can't see him. You can only experience his presence through the connection in your soul, where you experience an unexplained peace that is beyond understanding.

Spirituality vs. Religion

I am surprised that the topic of spirituality seems to bring about a level of discomfort despite that we are spiritual beings. We can talk about the mind and body all day with no issues, but when it comes to talking about spirituality, it seems as if people are afraid that they are going to say something offensive. There appears to be a pervasive fear of sharing one's spiritual beliefs, so much so that it has set many people on the course of silence and timidity.

So what does *spirit* really mean? One's spirit is the vital force that characterizes a human being as being alive. It is one's will or sense of self. Our bodies are designed to yearn after and seek a connection to a power source greater than ourselves. Spirit can also be thought of as one's soul or heart. It is *who* you are at the core or foundation of your being. It is also akin to your moral character, which comprises a variety of attributes, including integrity, courage, fortitude, honesty, loyalty, etc.

It is easy to confuse spirituality with religion, because religion is typically the focus of conversations, controversy, the media, and churches. Yet there is a distinct difference between the two.

Religion is an institutionalized system of beliefs and practices relating to the divine, including strongly held beliefs and opinions concerning worship of a deity. Because of this, religion itself will always leave room for division among people because of personal differences and preferences in how people choose to worship and what they choose to believe. The beliefs of different religions inspire such passion that they can divide families and cause disagreements, fights, and wars. People hate and even kill each other in the name of religion. But despite these negative consequences, the underlying factor of religious passion is that humans have a need to be connected to God—the one who created them—and will fight against anything that threatens or attacks their personal beliefs.

There are twenty major religions in the world, with upward of 4,000 variations of beliefs within them. Many variations of religions started with one person who had a different interpretation of a religion's dogma and had the leadership ability and skills to sell his or her ideas and opinions to others, and was then able to break off and form their own religion.

My faith, for example, is a variation of a major religion. Although I grew up in a traditionally Christian home, the particular belief system of the church I used to attend taught that those who belonged to that particular church and denomination were the only one true body of people who were "right" and would be able to go to heaven. While this thought seems obviously divisive and can breed superiority complexes, it was what I was taught and therefore became my religious belief. But as I got older and grew as an individual, my beliefs grew, too, and I learned to understand the difference between religion and spirituality. I learned that spirituality is more than your form of worship or the chosen methodology and beliefs that one individual may teach/preach about. It is about my personal relationship with God. Some people can be religious and get lost in their church's beliefs without having a personal connection with God. Being caught up in a system of beliefs of religion without having a relationship with God can leave one empty and void of understanding about the true essence of what you believe and why.

Spirituality and Why It's Necessary

Spirituality is often linked to the concept of a higher being—God or the divine—but people can hold sacred many other aspects of life. Dr. Kenneth Pargament, a prominent psychologist in the recent positive psychology movement, studied the effects of religion and spirituality on individuals and communities over a period of three decades, and his findings are quite fascinating. He defines spirituality as "a search for the sacred, an ever-evolving process of discovering, holding on to, and when necessary, transforming one's relationship with the sacred." He also proposes that "humans are yearning for a relationship with something sacred—something transcendent, boundless, and ultimate."

Dr. Pargament's research shows that those who are able to see the sacred in many aspects of their lives benefit both psychologically and physically (mind/body connection) and that religious involvement can help extend life expectancy. In addition, his research found that spiritual struggles and conflicts were linked to declines in mental and physical health, and shortened life spans. This shows why spirituality is crucial to our overall wellness.

Spirituality is the basis of your humanity, and it is imperative that your core is solid. Imagine if the foundation of your house was weak, had cracks, holes, or shifted too much. The weak foundation affected the structure and the strength of the rest of the house. It's the same with your spirit, which is the foundation of your being. Your morals, values, and character reside in the spiritual energy of who you are. If you have cracks and holes in your moral fiber, your life will be affected. How strong is your moral character? Your character, or who you are, is connected to your mind and determines how you think and behave.

The Need for Organized Religion

Although the focus of this chapter is spirituality, I do believe that it is important to explain the role that religion plays in spirituality. As I mentioned earlier, religion is defined as an institutionalized or personal system of beliefs and practices relating to the divine. Religion is an organized group of people who share like-minded beliefs, values, and styles of worship.

It is similar to all other membership-driven organizations. The camaraderie and emotions that may exist in any religious service is similar to the experience of fans of any sports team, for example, as well as other types of organizations. Recall Maslow's Hierarchy of Needs from Chapter 9: We all have a need to belong and to love, affiliate with others, and be accepted. The need to belong is ranked higher than even your self-esteem needs, because your self-esteem is enhanced by the love and acceptance that you feel from others.

You feel empowered, stable, and united when you are with others who feel, think, and believe the same way that you do. If religious services are coupled with your personal relationship with God, attending them can be experiences filled with a gamut of emotions. As the human soul is in tune with the vastness, power, and love of its Creator, it causes one to be filled with joy, admiration, respect, reverence, gratitude, and love simultaneously. The value of belonging to an organized religion include the feelings of importance and belonging; a sense of validation and unity with like-minded people; feelings of strength and boldness that comes with being a part of a crowd; opportunities to serve others; and a continual cycle of learning and personal growth. In essence, organized religion brings you an outside family structure that is meant to inspire, encourage, support, teach, and motivate you to be the best person that you can.

Can Spirituality Make You Happy?

If you're reading this book, you're likely seeking more happiness and fulfillment in your life. People often look to find happiness in money, materialistic things, or relationships. You have always heard the saying, "Money can't buy happiness." This maxim has truth because money itself is not what makes you happy. However, it can bring about a feeling of happiness because of what it affords you to do. You will need money in order to take the family vacation, but your family and the experiences that you have with them are what will ignite the feelings of pleasure and contentment. There is a distinct difference between pleasure and being content.

Some people seek happiness in things. They fill their lives with stuff. They purchase houses, cars, shoes, clothes, purses, jewelry, electronics, and gadgets in abundance, all because of a temporary feeling of pleasure that these acquisitions bring. A study conducted at San Francisco State University by Ryan Howell showed that life experiences rather than material possessions lead to greater happiness. Participants in the study were asked to write reflections and answer questions about their recent purchases. Participants indicated that experiential purchases represented money better spent and greater happiness for both themselves and others. The results also indicated that experiences produced more happiness regardless of the amount spent or the income of the consumer. For example, the feeling of happiness brought on by the purchase of theater or concert tickets may produce a greater sense of well-being than the purchase of things like furniture or clothes. Which makes sense because, according to Howell, experiences satisfy our need for "social connectedness and vitality—the feeling of being alive." Furthermore, experiences provide what researchers call "memory capital" that incubates long-term satisfaction. Howell explains, "We don't tend to get bored of happy memories like we do with a material object."

Meanwhile, other people look for happiness in their love interests. There is a false sense that another person will be able to bring you what you need to make you feel the sense of pleasure and contentment you desire. The truth is, while some people have the ability to bring about experiences that make you happy, true joy only comes from deep within your soul. It is about your sense of security, feeling of worth, and connection to God.

I have studied and worked with both types of people—spiritual, those claiming to have a personal connection to God or a higher power, and nonspiritual, those claiming not to have a personal connection to God. Spiritual people tend to be happier because their general outlook on life often involves more positivity. Although we all face the same problems as humans, having the connection to a higher source of power brings about a sense of peace. Spirituality seems to promote three areas that social scientists, researchers, and psychologists know improve our happiness: connections with others; a sense of purpose and meaning in our lives; and experiences of positive emotions.

REST STOP

In your notebook, answer the following questions:

1. When was the last time you felt happiness?
2. What was the experience that caused the feeling?
3. When was the last time you felt joy?
4. What was the experience that caused the feeling?
5. Are you looking for someone in life to bring you happiness?
6. Do you buy things in search of happiness?
7. Name three things that make you happy.

These questions will help you to look deep inside and understand what it is that makes you feel happy. It will help you understand if you are looking for it in things or people.

Connecting Spiritually

We have discussed spirituality, its value and benefits, and how it plays a major part in your overall well-being. In this section, we will review how to become spiritually connected. As with many things in your life, spiritual connectivity requires a conscious decision on your part. It starts with the recognition that your soul needs to be connected and in a relationship with God the Creator or another source of power greater than you. There are some steps and requirements that will facilitate this process and that will, in turn, help to generate joy and peace. One of the most important steps is clearing your heart from pain through the act of forgiveness.

The Art of Forgiveness

Forgiveness is by far one of the most difficult missions to accomplish. It is the act of pardoning someone for a mistake or wrongdoing. To pardon means to officially *release* somebody who has committed a crime or offense from further punishment. The natural psychological responses to being hurt, offended, disappointed, betrayed, embarrassed, disrespected, mislead, deceived, snubbed, or injured is to defend or protect one's self. Your mind, body, and spirit are all affected and respond accordingly. Being wronged by someone results in some of the most horrible feelings that you can experience. A rush of negative emotions will flood your mind and body at the same time. When you are experiencing these emotions, the act and feeling of love takes a back seat. In preparing to defend, shield, and protect your heart, you will put up a road block to keep others from reaching you.

While this defensive strategy is a natural response, several things happen when you don't deal with the issue and the person who has wronged you by extending forgiveness. Here is a visual of what happens when unforgiveness remains in your spirit: You will build walls. On the inside of the walls, there are at least three buckets. One bucket is filled with anger, one with hurt, and one with resentment. The longer you hold on to those feelings, the longer they remain in the bucket and begin to change into deeper feelings. The anger changes to bitterness, hurt becomes intense pain, and resentment turns into hatred. Remember, these buckets are closed up behind the wall you built, so the toxicity of these thoughts and feelings will start to create a foul odor that permeates your mind, body, and spirit. You may become consumed with revenge and hatred, and ultimately unforgiveness will begin to take over your mind, control your actions, and disintegrate your spirit. Meanwhile, keep in mind that the person or people who hurt you are on the outside of this wall. They are living their life. Oftentimes, they have moved on and have no clue about the poison that has taken over your body. You are miserable; they are not.

In Chapter 9, we dealt with hurt and pain and established that when pain is not properly managed, hurt people *hurt* people. And sometimes the ways they hurt are through all types of appalling events. Through my line of work, I have heard about cases of rape, incest, molestation, abuse, abandonment, infidelity, murder, theft, abduction, and more. Even with these types of horrific tragedies, I highly encourage individuals to move toward the act of forgiveness. Understanding that it is a process that takes time, forgiveness is the road to becoming healthy and taking back your power that someone may have stolen from you. It lifts the heavy weight from you and allows you to move forward without being haunted with past negativity.

According to some studies done at Duke University, forgiving those who have wronged you can also help lower blood pressure, cholesterol, and heart rate. At Duke University, researchers report a strong correlation between forgiveness and strengthened immunity among HIV-positive patients. Forgiveness is also associated with improved sleep quality, which has a strong effect on health. Of course, the benefits are not just limited to the body. Letting go of bitterness and resentment reduces levels of depression, anxiety, and anger. People who learn to forgive tend to have better relationships, feel happier and more optimistic, and enjoy an overall better psychological well-being.

While there is no single method or magic to forgiving, the techniques I suggest in the following section will help you on the road to recovery. The most difficult incidents for me to let go of and to forgive were the doctors killing my son and the jury deciding they should not be punished. In the midst of grieving over losing my children, I had to deal with the anger stemming from knowing that they lied and got away with taking a life, even if it was accidental. While I did not wish the doctors any harm, I began to develop resentment. It was only after I found it in my heart to forgive them that I was able to find a measure of peace with the situation. Following are the steps I recommend both professionally and personally that will enable you to forgive.

ROAD TO FORGIVENESS

1. **Acknowledge and express your emotions.** Allow yourself to feel the anger, pain, confusion, anxiety, etc. Find a safe place to release your emotions. It may be in a confidant, family member, pastor, or counselor.

2. **Write down your feelings.** I always recommend writing. It is very cathartic. It helps to see things clearly in words on a page. It helps you to process the event in a different way.

3. **Make a decision.** Decide that you are going to take your life back and get rid of the buckets of poison inside your wall. As discussed, you have to make a decision that you want to be successful and take control of your life. Making a decision to forgive is powerful and full of benefits for your health. As discussed in Chapter 2, when you make a decision, your body will align itself to do what is necessary to help you forgive.

4. **Focus on the action and not the person.** Make sure that you concentrate your efforts on the act itself as opposed to the person who wronged you. Many times we are more hurt because of who committed the offense rather than what they did. The emotions surrounding *who* did it can be even more painful than *what* they did. I know that you can feel different levels of pain when, say, your brother betrays you versus when a virtual stranger betrays you. But focusing on the hurtful action itself rather than the person can help you maintain perspective and remove personal animosity from the equation.

5. **If possible, communicate your feelings to the person you seek to forgive.** This is helpful if it is possible to let the person know how you feel. For psychological reasons, it makes you feel better to be able to confront them and express your feelings. It may also help you answer the "Why did you do it?" question that always taunts the mind.

6. **Let it go.** Consciously choose to give up your role as a victim. This is a process that requires you to create your own closure.

Sometimes this healing process may require that you write a letter to the offender, one that you send as a final gesture of pardon or that you write and tear up. It will require that you block the negative thoughts about the incident when it comes back to your mind. Replace it with words of affirmation.

7. **Set your boundaries**. This step is important to do to protect yourself from any repeat offenses. Make sure that you know specifically what you will not tolerate.

8. **Write down your lessons**. Write down the lessons that you learned from this particular experience. This helps you to focus on the positive things that have come from this experience instead of the negative.

9. **Pray**. Praying can be useful for strength and guidance. Some things can only be done through the extra strength you get when you are spiritually connected. Forgiveness is one of them.

Is there someone you need to forgive? How long have you been holding on to the poison? Write down the person to whom you need to give the gift of forgiveness. Using the steps suggested above, begin your process today to cut loose the grudges and the dead weight. When you forgive, you are granting someone pardon and release—but the biggest gift is to you.

Finding Your Purpose

Knowing and understanding your purpose in life, or reason for existing, is a critical piece of spirituality. It helps you to live life with intent, because you know what your job is here on the planet. Imagine that your job was to dig a hole that was thirty feet wide and five feet deep. You worked and worked every day to get the job done. It took you three months to finally complete the job. And then, your boss told you that now your new job was to refill the hole with the same dirt you had dug up. This arduous, seemingly meaningless task is what your life is like when you don't know your purpose for being alive. You are living life each day routinely, doing the same things day in and day out, and not understanding your "assignment" or that you were born for a reason bigger than you are.

Do you know the reason that you were born? What is the assignment that you are to fulfill while you are alive? As I travel around the country to speak, I ask members of the audience to raise their hands if they know their purpose. Consistently only 5 to 10 percent of an audience will raise their hands.

In 2002, Rick Warren wrote a book entitled *The Purpose Driven Life*. The focus of the book was to help people live a life of purpose. Other spiritual leaders, too, discuss how to find and live your purpose. Yet despite the message that's been widely preached—Warren's book, for example, has reportedly sold thirty million copies—I have found that the majority of the people I poll still do not have a clue as to what their purpose is. Many people are on a journey in which they're living life with no clear direction. It leaves people vulnerable when they wander aimlessly to whatever place sounds great; when they spend energy on things that are a waste of time; when they say yes to things they can't handle; or, when they have no real meaning or focus in their lives.

There are more than seven billion people on earth, and there is a reason why each of us exists. Each person has an assignment to carry out, and it may take some digging to figure out what it is. Sometimes it's easier to see someone else's purpose because of their fame—Celine Dion's purpose is to bless people through song, Oprah Winfrey's is to encourage and inspire women to be authentic and listen to their inner selves. Most people aren't meant to become famous while fulfilling their purpose, but finding and living your purpose will lead you to a more meaningful life. It will enable you to have a different perspective of the challenges that will come your way and it will allow you to live life with intention. If you would like more information on finding your purpose, go to www.creatingamazinglives.com and click on "Purpose."

REST STOP

In your notebook, write the answers to these questions.

1. Do you know the reason that you were born? If so, why were you born?
2. Have you created a mission statement for your life? If not, write your life mission.
3. Are you acting out your purpose in your daily life?

If you have found, while on your journey, that you feel that you need to work on your spiritual growth, the following tips will help you to increase your spiritual awareness and level.

Road to Spirituality

1. Begin your day with prayer or meditation.
2. Learn the art of forgiveness.
3. End your day with a word of thanks.
4. Encapsulate the spirit of gratitude, not greed.
5. Know that there is a reason why you exist and seek to find it.
6. Practice the virtues of faith, hope, and love.
7. Seek to make someone smile every day.
8. Treat others the way you wish to be treated.
9. Schedule at least thirty minutes a day for yourself.

Having an amazing life requires having an amazing spirit. Finding the peace on your journey is an everyday practice. The following tips, when integrated into your life, will help you continue to create an amazing life on this journey, in spite of your circumstances and life events. Know that spirituality and faith adds so many benefits to your health, happiness, and longevity.

Roadmap

Embracing your spirituality.

1. **Recognize and acknowledge there is a greater power.** The first step to strengthening your spirituality is to understand that there is an existing power that is greater than you. Although there may be different names that people choose to call God, it is the same true knowledge and recognition that there is a source that is greater than you.

2. **Walk in faith.** You have to understand that believing in the divine requires faith—the belief and confidence that somebody or something exists even though you can't see it.

3. **Acknowledge your weakness.** Know and understand that you have human frailties and limitations of knowledge. When you can admit your weaknesses and acknowledge His power, it leaves room for faith to take over.

4. **Pursue a relationship with God.** As we have learned, the key to a successful relationship is staying connected, and behaving in a way that the other person knows, believes, and feels that you love and care for him or her. The same ideals should be applied to your relationship with God. It is critical to make deliberate choices every day that will help you in your relationship with God.

5. **Pray.** Prayer is a spoken or unspoken address to God, a deity, or a saint. It may express praise, thanksgiving, a confession, or a

request for something, such as help or somebody's well-being. It is important to address God daily.

6. **Seek to love.** If someone has no love, he or she tends to be more depressed and lonely, and doesn't necessarily function well in society. Because God is love, when you are connected to him, you experience an overwhelming sense of affection and security. He asks that we share our love with each other.

7. **Live in gratitude.** Approach each day with gratitude. Being grateful for what you have and who you are. It is easy to look at what you don't have instead of focusing on what you do. A grateful heart will bring about a peaceful spirit.

8. **Seek to know your purpose.** Review the last section in this chapter, visit my Web site, and really think about your purpose. When you are walking in your purpose, you feel alive and "found," not lost.

9. **Respect yourself and others.** Treat yourself with respect at all times. Don't allow others to disrespect you. When you love who you are and have set clear boundaries, you will make certain that they are adhered to.

10. **Smile.** It shows that you are happy on the inside.

THIRTEEN

Stop Signs, Red Lights, and Blinking Yellows

Slowing Down to Enjoy the Moment

P ICTURE YOURSELF behind the wheel, with the road stretching in front of you. Now, let me ask you, are you driving the speed limit or are you driving faster? Are you always in a hurry to reach your destination?

It's easy to always be in the fast lane, both on the freeway and in life. We live in a culture that is filled with deadlines, schedules, programs, calendars, alarms, activities, meetings, dinners, games, courses, webinars, conference calls, events, conferences, retreats, and on and on. I must constantly remind myself to slow down. We need to be mindful of getting to our destination, something this book has discussed in great deal, but we also have to enjoy the journey itself. That's what this chapter is about.

Seize the Moment

Living in the moment is essential to your emotional health. Since I am the emotional wellness doctor, I am observed everywhere I go; people are always curious to see how emotionally healthy I look and act. So I've worked hard to master the art of learning how to manage my emotions and live in the moment. While it may appear as though my life is stress free, it comes down to making deliberate choices to be emotionally healthy every day. In this chapter, I will share my secrets for letting go of the past and not worrying about the future. These are simple techniques for being in the moment and being fully present.

Letting Go of the Past

Do any of these comment(s) play on repeat in your head?

- "I can't seem to forget what happened to me when I was growing up."
- "No matter what I do, when I think about what she/he said, I get angry all over again."
- "I wish I would have said NO. Now look at what has happened."
- "I should have taken that job. I wouldn't be in this financial mess."
- "I wish I would have fought back."
- "I wish I wouldn't have fought back."

Many of those 60,000 thoughts that are running around in your mind daily have to do with the past, or with the future. You are either dwelling on or replaying events; feeling guilt or remorse about something you did, or should have done; or you're worrying about, calculating, daydreaming, wishing, or projecting into the future. How much of your time do you think you spend "in the moment"? Well, I can tell you that very little of your time is spent in the moment *unless* you are conscientious of living in the moment. It's a decision we must make.

Being in the moment became extremely important for me when I was going through my divorce. As difficult as things may have been, I couldn't afford to be on stage speaking in front of an organization, or administering training, looking like life had beaten me up. We all face challenges, but it's important to learn how to not carry them with us everywhere we go. In order to accomplish living in the moment, we first have to learn how to release the past.

Why is the past so hard to let go of? The past is all about memories, both good and bad. The good memories become the things that you want to hold onto. They are what make you smile, warm your heart, promote conversation, and allow you to develop history. Sometimes, it is hard to move on from those memories. You can also be haunted by painful memories that can haunt your present and tarnish your future. Some of the painful memories that you may carry from the past could include abuse, neglect, rape, death, and illness. These are things that were forced into your life. These types of events carry a different psychological effect than the bad choices you made that in turn became bad memories. When there is something that you have no control over, it takes away your power to make choices for your life. This can leave you feeling powerless and hopeless.

The people who chose to fight the uncontrollable life events carry the harmful memories around with them in everyday life. In an attempt to control the present and future, they may have anger, resentment, or operate in a defensive mode. They either think that everyone is out to get them, or they lack the ability to trust people. The people that run from the past still carry the memories with them, but they have been neatly tucked away. They believe that not talking about it creates a nonexistence of the reality. While they may appear to be fine, there are things in the present that can trigger the memories. There is a certain level of vulnerability that surrounds them, that attracts the same type of destruction to occur in the present.

You can also become preoccupied with regrets from the past, feeling shame, pain, frustration, etc., with decisions that you have made in life. While I talked extensively in Chapter 12 about forgiveness, it was focused on forgiving others. But forgiving yourself is just as important. Not healing from your past and not forgiving yourself can affect your self-esteem, create insecurities, depression, and cause emotional stress.

ROAD TO FORGIVING YOURSELF

1. Acknowledge that the choice you made was not the best one.
2. Take responsibility for the choice and the consequences that have followed. Don't become a victim or blame someone else for your life.
3. Understand that every human makes mistakes. You are not alone.
4. Talk to a trusted friend, counselor, or clergy member about your mistakes/past. This person can offer advice that will help you feel better and have a more positive outlook.
5. If you have wronged someone, try to apologize. Remember that is your job, but you can't control the outcome: it is up to the other person to forgive you.
6. Write a list of lessons you learned from the experience.
7. Let go of the guilt and shame.
8. Love yourself. Continue to repeat poet Maya Angelou's words, "When you know better, you do better."
9. Ask God for forgiveness, and know he will extend it to you.

To help you leave behind the past, think of it as the school of life. Do you remember high school? There was so much to learn, and so many new opportunities. You went to class every day, and you made the choice whether you wanted to listen, learn, do your homework, and study. The teacher's job was to present you with the lesson every day. What you did with it was up to you. Your past is a form of school. It is a mixture of electives and mandatory core classes. Some of your experiences were chosen, and others were required. Your required experiences help to build the foundation of who you would become. Understand that while you don't get to choose the things that will mold and shape you, they do happen for a reason. The reason, while it may not have made sense to you at the time, was in preparation for your future.

If you look at your past as the school of learning, you will be able to work through it with a better perspective. Everything is a lesson.

It is time to look at the steps to release and free yourself from the past memories that are holding you back from having an amazing life.

ROAD TO LETTING GO OF THE PAST

1. Write down the event/person you would like to release. Be as specific as possible. It may be several events, or people, that you want to let go.
2. Write down your regrets about the experience. Was it choices that you made, lack of control of the situation, a relationship that was toxic, a betrayal, etc.?
3. Accept that you can't change the past, only learn from it.
4. Write down your lessons.
5. Focus on the good memories from the experience.
6. Turn your learning into something positive.
7. Volunteer your time.
8. Comfort others with your lessons.

Worrying about the Future

Have you heard of the term "worry wart"? Worry is another emotion that inhabits our mind, body, and spirit. When we worry we have thoughts, images, and feelings of a negative nature about *anticipated* events and challenges. These thoughts generally surround a person's finances, health, relationships, kids, or the economy. Some worrying is a natural part of the human process. There are situations that are normal to fret about: will my new boss like me? Will a date be impressed with me? Will my husband like my new haircut? However, excessive worrying can cause high anxiety—even panic attacks. Many chronic worriers describe a feeling of impending doom or unrealistic fears that only increase their worries. Being ultrasensitive to one's environment and to the criticism of others, excessive worriers may see anything—and anyone—as a potential threat. Constant worrying affects not only your personal life, but it interferes with your appetite, lifestyle habits, relationships, sleep, and job performance. It can also lead to self-destructive behaviors like overeating, cigarette smoking, or alcohol or drug abuse.

So how do we deal with anxiety? As discussed in detail in Chapter 9, anxiety is a normal reaction to stress. Ongoing anxiety, though, may be the result of a disorder such as generalized anxiety disorder, panic disorder, or social anxiety. Anxiety disorders affect nearly forty million adults in the United States. Your body reacts chemically to the "fear" that worrying can create. When you are afraid, your body releases adrenalin. This results in the "fight or flight" reflex that we experience to help us to battle or run away from anything that threatens us physically. Adrenalin affects the digestive system, and can make you feel ill. The more you worry, the worse it gets, and a sudden rush of adrenalin can lead to butterflies in the stomach, a headache, or feeling very sick.

If you're a parent, worry becomes a part of your DNA. No one warns you that becoming a parent comes with its official bag of worry and guilt. It's filled with all sorts of should'ves, could'ves, would'ves from the second your children are born all the way through adulthood. There is plenty to worry about, but you need to manage the worries so that you don't drive yourself crazy. I do believe that as women we have been given an extra gift called intuition, which is even more pronounced when it comes to your children. In my work, I have given advice to many mothers who have been caught up in the worry-and-guilt cycle, worried about what their kids will do/not do, and guilty because of the things they have done. They are either consumed with something in their children's past or worried about their future. Because of this, it inhibits them from living and enjoying the moment. I would like to share a story of one of my clients who has every right and reason to be haunted by her past and worried about the future but has been able to overcome them both. I have worked with so many people over the course of my profession, yet no one made the impression on me or taught me so many lessons along the way as Mary.

Mary is a quiet woman with a soft-spoken voice and a demeanor that belies the pain and sorrow she has experienced. She grew up in a house with an extremely emotionally abusive father. As a teenager, instead of hanging out with friends, she had to help care for her brother, a quadriplegic. At seventeen, she got married to escape that life. That marriage didn't last, but she found love again. Between the two marriages, she was blessed with five beautiful children. While her children were young, Mary's mother began to develop Alzheimer's and the responsibility of her care fell on Mary. Meanwhile, her middle son Tommy was hit by a car at the age of four and was left a quadriplegic. This unimaginable horror, pain, and guilt haunted her and his siblings. Amid this turmoil, she discovered that her second husband was addicted to drugs, which caused extreme discord and wreaked havoc in her home. Her life consisted of being a single mother, working full time while caring regularly for her mother as well as her brother on the weekends, and of course her son, who required round-the-clock care.

When she lost her mother and brother, she had no time to grieve because she was still busy caring for her son and dealing with her husband's addiction. Fast-forward a few years. Her son Tommy was introduced to marijuana and her youngest son attempted suicide. She found out soon after that he had been molested at an early age. Then her husband died of an overdose. Just when she thought she couldn't handle any more, Tommy was arrested for possession of marijuana. Even though he was a first-time offender, and in need of round-the-clock care, he was sentenced to ten days in jail. The jail knew he needed a ventilator in order to breathe at night, but they didn't have one available. Mary and her attorney fought to have his breathing machine brought to jail, but by the time they got it approved, on his fourth day of incarceration, he died of respiratory complications. Her storms continued to rage as her oldest and youngest battled with drug addiction. While the oldest is in recovery and is taking life one day at a time, the youngest is still fighting for his life.

When she came to me, Mary had experienced many dark nights filled with tears, mornings filled with the dread of facing another day, and the feeling of helplessness and unbearable heavy sadness that encircled her spirit. She and I dealt one by one with all of the pain, anger, hurt, betrayal, disbelief, shock, guilt, terror, and the numb feelings that had become so familiar to her. While I was able to guide her through a process of recovery, her mental and physical strength that kept her grounded was because of her spiritual connection. In her case, her spirituality enabled her to get through her life without her choosing to medicate her pain through addictions or rage. The hardest part of the process was learning how to let go of the past that affected her thoughts of the future. Today, Mary is doing well and enjoys being a grandmother. She is retired and working on her second phase of life. Her desire is to return to school to become a certified counselor so that she can help others work through the adversity that life can bring. She stopped worrying about the future and has learned how to plan for the future.

ROAD TO STOP WORRYING

1. Write down a list of your worries. Put them in categories based upon situations, people, health, and finances.
2. After you have your worry list, put an x beside those things on the list that you have any control over. For example, while you cannot control choices someone you love makes, you can control your own finances and health.
3. Accept that worrying about the things on your list that you cannot control will not change the outcome. You are wasting energy, thoughts, and time.
4. Focus your energy on the things on your list you can control. For example, review Chapters 10 and 11 to create a plan for your finances and your health.
5. Refocus your thoughts and nervous energy into a hobby.

Living in the Present

At this exact moment, where are you reading this book? Are you in your house in your favorite room, in a waiting room, at the office, outdoors, in a bookstore, on an airplane, or somewhere else? Stop a second and look at your surroundings. What do you see? Are there other people in your presence? Are there trees, flowers, or grass? Look at the people/ objects. Notice the colors, shapes, and textures. Now concentrate on you. Take note of your breathing. Are you taking deep breaths or are they shallow? Take a slow deep breath. Did you feel your lungs expand? Learning how to live in the moment requires very conscious efforts of present day and moment living. There is constant motion and a barrage of stimulus that is all around us. We are inundated with technology, entertainment, social media, etc. With so much constant stimulation, how is it possible to live in the moment? Again, it is a very conscious choice that you have to make to be in your present space. It also requires taking the time to program your brain for it.

So much of life passes us by while we are thinking or talking about what we have done, or what we are planning to do. So many people actually *miss* their lives because they aren't in the present. I am certain that you have been around those people who seem unengaged in your conversation, distracted by their own thoughts, to-do list, or smart phone. You can tell that they are definitely not in the present. Commit to becoming a person who not only lives in the moment, but enjoys it.

ROAD TO BEING IN THE MOMENT

1. **Give undivided attention to what you are doing.** Try to keep your focus on the task at hand until it is complete. This also includes conversations. Listen attentively, without trying to think of what you want to say.

2. **Be content to be where you are.** If you are attending a meeting that you would have rather skipped, work to be comfortable in that space. Tell your brain that you are satisfied and you want to learn something new. It will help you to focus in the moment.

3. **Practice talking about the present.** Share what is happening right now, your thoughts and feelings.

4. **Set a schedule to accomplish tasks in a way in which you can avoid distractions.**

5. **Make a conscious effort to enjoy where you are and what you are doing.** Avoid carrying your issues with you. Leave them home. I guarantee they will be waiting for you when you get back.

6. **Focus on your breathing.** It puts you in the moment.

7. **Be aware and take note of your surroundings.** This is also helpful in terms of personal safety. Many attacks happen because people are distracted and not in the moment.

8. **Take time to stop and smell the roses.** Make sure that you focus on the things that are important in life.

Although there is no life-management class that you are required to take to "do life," I have given you many tools to create an amazing life. Your journey is different and unique from anyone else's and it should be planned uniquely for you. Your programming doesn't and shouldn't work for anyone else. Just as unique as your fingerprint, so is your life. As the driver of your life, you have control of your direction, speed, routes, maintenance, lane travel, exits, U-turns, rest stop, and destination. While I believe that God is in ultimate control of the world and how the streets of our life are laid out, we are given power to make choices as to how we want to live.

REST STOP

For the last time, I would like you to get out your notebook and reflect over your life. Answer these questions:

1. Are you living in the present?
2. Are you living your life to the fullest?

Write down at least five ways that you can practice living in the present.

Now that we have gone through each of the chapters, I would like for you to revisit your answers to the questions posed in Chapter 2:

1. Where are you now?
2. Where would you like to be?
3. What will it take for you to get there?

You may need to modify your answers now that you have been given many tools and strategies. Continue to utilize this book and your notebook as it is your roadmap to creating your amazing life.

Lexi's Story

In this book, I have shared many tips, techniques, strategies, facts, stories, and lessons that will help you become the person you were meant to be. I shared stories from others, as well as personal stories from my own life. I felt it was important that you know that I have had challenges, roadblocks, detours, accidents, and flat tires, just like everyone else.

And as I have offered you lessons and insights from my journey, I too have had teachers along the way. One of the best is my youngest daughter, Lexi. She has been her own person from day one. While I could not quite put my finger on it, I knew that she was different from the other children. She had a mind and a will of iron. When she was eight months, it became clear just how strong willed she was. While she was crawling around, she started playing with one of the plants. Sensing danger, I said to her, "No, no, don't touch the plant." She ignored me and touched it again. This time I repeated with a firm voice, "No, no, Mommy said don't touch the plant."

Having four children, I was not a novice at parenting. The process is as follows: tell your kids what to do and they obey. But the process wasn't working with Lexi. To my dismay, she touched the plant again. *She doesn't realize I am the boss, and that she is supposed to do what I say,* I thought. To get her attention, I tapped her fingers. My eyes and voice were stern as I pointed my finger and said, "No, no. Do not touch the plant!"

It was decision time. She looked at her hand, at me, and then the plant. When she touched the plant again, I knew that I was in trouble and called my mother. That was just the beginning. Her colorful life filled our lives with surprise, laughter, disbelief, and forced us to reinvent our rules and consequences. Lexi has taught me a lot about the journey. When she was three years old, I wrote down some valuable lessons that have become a guide for life that I want to leave with you.

Roadmap

Lessons from Lexi:

1. **Know what you want and when you want it.** There was never a question in her mind of what she wanted. She knew what she wanted to eat, wear, watch, listen to, and do. She knew exactly

what she wanted and when she wanted it. From day one, Lexi has been in the driver's seat of her life.

2. **Speak honestly.** She never hesitated to tell me if she didn't like something, or if my breath smelled funny. Be honest with yourself and others. Speak the truth in love.

3. **Plan your course of action.** Every night she had a plan as to how she would avoid going to bed. You could actually see the wheels of her mind turning as she planned creative excuses to avoid bedtime. Some nights it was a sore throat or headache; she was thirsty; she bumped her arm, etc. Just like Lexi, you have to plan out your life and your course of action. It will require creative thinking and strategy to chart how you will reach your destination.

4. **Admit when you're wrong.** When she did something wrong, she would always tell me, "Mommy, look what I did!" Even at the tender age of three, she learned she would get in less trouble if she admitted that she was wrong so she could get empathy and forgiveness, instead of lying and getting in trouble. Learn how to admit when you are wrong. Take responsibilities for your actions. It is easier to be forgiven when you own up to your "stuff."

5. **Get angry, let it out, and move on.** Lexi would get upset at her siblings, cry, and then two minutes later it was like nothing had happened. She would have forgotten that she was upset a few minutes earlier. Practice acknowledging your emotions and releasing them in a safe place. When you have released them, move forward. Don't hang on to your emotions, because they can cause stress. It's like the kids say: Build a bridge and get over it.

6. **Let the simple things make you happy and learn to laugh.** She loved to laugh. She would get so excited over the smallest things. Getting a ring from the candy machine would make her day. What does it take to make you happy? Get back to enjoying the simple things of life. Go for a walk. Get some ice cream topped with gummy bears. Returning to the innocence of a child is a good thing. Children really know how to be happy.

7. **Believe you can do everything**. She wanted to and believed that she could do everything. "Mommy, let me do it," she'd say, and "I can do it." This really bothered me. Since she was the last one, I wanted to keep her a baby for as long as I could. She, on the other hand, pushed to do everything on her own. She believed in herself. Just think of how much you could accomplish if you truly believed in yourself. Believe it in your mind and your heart will feel it, your hands will do it, and your spirit will rejoice in it.

Thank you for letting me share my life and gifts with you. We are all on this journey together. I wish you all the best on your journey to creating your amazing life. My mission is to help you get there any way that I can. For more information on my programs and resources that I offer, go to www.creatingamazinglives.com. Here's to your amazing life!

Acknowledgments

A S WITH ANY JOURNEY OF LIFE, there are many people that help you reach your destination, such was the case with this book project. It took a collaboration of a collective body of people to make this happen—some who have had confidence and belief in my vision, others who have the skill set to make things happen, and of course there are those cheerleaders that have rooted for me until the very end.

Let me begin thanking my publisher, BenBella, for seeing the vision for this book and giving me the opportunity to share my gift to the world. A special thank you is extended to Cheryl Carr for being the person who began to connect the dots for the vision and the people who could make it happen. Thank you to Raoul Davis, my agent, for taking a risk and believing that this project could soar to great heights and opening doors to make it happen. Also, I extend my gratitude to Leticia Gomez, who came on board and introduced me to a new world of contacts and helped to prepare me for what is to come.

Thank you to Christine Pride, my editor, who through her gift of writing helped make me a better writer. And Debbie Harmsen, Vy Tran, and Alexis Kelly, who helped to sand and polish all of the loose ends to ensure an excellent finished product. To my business associates, Veronica and Michael, who encouraged me to write the book with urgency and to grab this title and run with it. To my mentor, Myron Golden, who has taught me so much and stretched my thinking to encompass big thoughts and dreams.

A distinctive thank you goes to my mother, Shirley. You have always been there for me and supported me on all of my journeys. Your encouragement, love, and prayers have provided the stable rock that I stand on. You have guided me, listened, encouraged, challenged, and loved me through it all. To my siblings, Sarita, Tina, Theresa, and Isaac, thank you for your unconditional love and family bond.

I am eternally grateful to my sister friends, who are my lifelong cheerleaders: Jacqueline, Sandra, Anita, and Tracy. Over the last thirty years, you have given encouragement, friendship, support, love, and laughter, and challenged and motivated me to be the best, as well as cheered for me through this project. You have been there in my corner through the detours, construction, delays, jams, tears, and happiness. To my newer sister friends, Kristee and Camille, your faithful and loyal friendship has helped me to reach for my destiny. Thank you for your thoughts and ideas for this project.

An exceptional thanks goes out to all my beautiful children, Jordan, Bria, Jazzy, and Lexi. You are truly the light of my life and help me to be the best woman I can. You bring me indescribable joy, and the love I have for you continues to grow each day.

Finally, I give all praise and honor to God, for his blessings and gifts that he has given me to give back to the world. He makes all things possible!

About the Author

D R. GLADNEY is not just the "Emotional Wellness Doctor"; she is also a speaker, trainer, and CEO of her own company, Emotional Wellness. She speaks to companies, schools, and churches, and has worked with many Fortune 500 companies and clients, including IBM, Pitney Bowes, AT&T, Aetna, Brinker International, Freddie Mac, Texas Instruments, and the U.S. Department of Defense. She has also presented speeches and training sessions internationally. She has earned many honors in her career and continues to be a trailblazer in the area of health and wellness.

She is a television personality and has been a cohost of a cable show and a residential expert for *Insights* on Fox 4 in Dallas. As an emotional wellness expert, Dr. Gladney has been interviewed on national TV and radio shows, reaching more than twenty-two million people with her message. She has written articles and books that help people manage their emotions and stress, thereby creating their amazing lives. She is the mother of four children.